Sweet Dreams Princess

Bedtime Bible Stories, Devotions, & Prayers

PRESENTED TO

PRESENTED BY

DATE

OCCASION

Sweet Dreams Princess
Bedtime Bible Stories, Devotions & Prayers

General Editor: Sheila Walsh
Gigi, God's Little Princess™ illustrations copyright © 2005 by Sheila Walsh
Illustrator: Meredith Johnson

Published in Nashville, Tennessee, by Thomas Nelson, Inc.

Typeset, design and spot art by: Koechel Peterson & Associates, Inc., Minneapolis, MN
Editorial Team: Jennifer Morgan Gerelds, writer; Beverly Riggs, editor

Printed in China
1 2 3 4 5 – 12 11 10 09 08

Sweet Dreams Princess

God's Little Princess®

Bedtime Bible Stories, Devotions, & Prayers

Sheila Walsh

International Children's Bible

THOMAS NELSON
Since 1798

For other products and live events,
visit us at: **thomasnelson.com**

Dear Princess,

Before you close your eyes and say goodnight to another day, I want to remind you of some wonderful news!

Do you know that just as you are, right at this very moment, you are loved and treasured by God? Even if today wasn't such a good day and you feel a little sad or a little mad, God loves you so much and you can tell him how you feel. Every day with God is a new beginning and every evening is an opportunity to take a few moments to say, "Thank you for loving me and watching over me."

It is my prayer for you, Princess, that you will go to sleep with a big smile tucked inside you because you are special. You are God's Little Princess!

Your Big Sister,

Sheila

Contents

Dear Parents and Princesses,

This wonderful new Bible storybook includes scripture stories taken right from the International Children's Bible® translation, the first version created especially for children. Each of these classic and well-known favorite Bible stories is accompanied by a devotion from Sheila Walsh and closes with a Prayer, Promise or Praise.

The Prayers are a great way for little princesses to start developing the wonderful habit of talking with God through prayer at the close of their day.

The Promises are a short note just for your tired little princess to know that she can count on God's promises every day and every night. God's love is never-ending, and he will always be there for your princess!

The Praises are a starter for princesses to think about the blessings in their life and praise God for them. It's a wonderful way to help her see the good things and acknowledge them in prayer and praise.

We hope this Bible storybook will create a fun bedtime experience for you and your God's little princess to enjoy for years to come!

The Publisher

Sweet Dreams Princess

Bedtime Bible Stories, Devotions, & Prayers

God Makes the World

GENESIS 1:1-5, 9-11, 14, 16-17

In the beginning God created the sky and the earth. The earth was empty and had no form. Darkness covered the ocean, and God's Spirit was moving over the water.

Then God said, "Let there be light!" And there was light. God saw that the light was good. So he divided the light from the darkness. God named the light "day" and the darkness "night."…

Then God said, "Let the water under the sky be gathered together so the dry land will appear." And it happened. God named the dry land "earth." He named the water that was gathered together "seas." God saw that this was good.

Then God said, "Let the earth produce plants. Some plants will make grain for seeds. Others will make fruit with seeds in it. Every seed will produce more of its own kind of plant." And it happened....

Then God said, "Let there be lights in the sky to separate day from night....

So God made the two large lights. He made the brighter light to rule the day. He made the smaller light to rule the night. He also made the stars. God put all these in the sky to shine on the earth.

creation

Sweet Dreams Devotion

Are you ready for sleep, Princess? Okay, close your eyes. Are they shut tightly? What can you see? It's very dark, isn't it? It was even darker when God decided to make our world. So the first thing God said was, "Let there be light!" And the darkness disappeared! Lit up like a million sparkling jewels, the earth began to take shape as God spoke it into being. Water separated from sky. The sun and moon were put into place. Plants, animals, and the first people appeared. It was just how God wanted it to be. Everything was perfect in his care. Do you know that you are always in God's care? God would never take his eyes off his little Princess, now would he?

 So, if you are ever afraid of the dark, don't be! God sees just as well in the dark as he does in the light. He holds you close to his heart in the day and the night. So, sweet dreams, Princess!

Promise

God made everything, even me! He knows just how to take care of me.

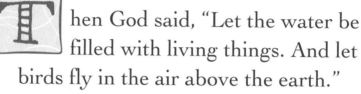

God Makes the Animals

GENESIS 1:20-25

Then God said, "Let the water be filled with living things. And let birds fly in the air above the earth."

So God created the large sea animals. He created every living thing that moves in the sea. The sea is filled with these living things. Each one produces more of its own kind. God also made every bird that flies. And each bird produces more if its own kind. God saw that this was good. God blessed them and said, "Have many young ones and grow in number. Fill the water of the seas, and let the birds grow in number on the earth." Evening passed, and morning came. This was the fifth day.

Then God said, "Let the earth be filled with animals. And let each produce more its own kind. Let there be tame animals and small crawling animals and wild animals. And let each produce more if its kind." And it happened.

So God made the wild animals, the tame animals and all the small crawling animals to produce more of their own kind. God saw that this was good.

animals

Sweet Dreams Devotion

What's your favorite animal? Is it the elephant, with its funny, long trunk? How about a cute, little bunny hopping across a field? Or perhaps you like the panda, with its fuzzy face and love for bamboo shoots. It's hard to have a favorite with so many animals to choose from. Have you met Gigi, God's little Princess? She loves her cat, Lord Fluffy, and her sweet little dog, Tiarra. Isn't it amazing how creative God is? How did he think up so many wonderful ideas? Not only did he make animals for the earth, he also put them in the sky and the ocean too. Everywhere we look, we find his creatures living, playing, and showing us the proof that God is wiser and more powerful than anyone else on earth.

How can you be sure that God is real? Take a look at the incredible creation around you. Then take a look in the mirror and see what a perfect little Princess he made when he made you! Let's thank God for his creativity and power.

PRAISE:

Dear God, I **PRAISE** you
for your amazing love.
No one is as powerful,
CREATIVE, or wonderful as you!

Adam and Eve Tempted

 ow the snake was the most clever of all the wild animals the Lord God had made. One day the snake spoke to the woman. He said, "Did God really say that you must not eat fruit from any tree in the garden?"

The woman answered the snake, "We may eat fruit from the trees in the garden. But God told us, 'You must not eat fruit from the tree that is in the middle of the garden. You must not even touch it, or you will die.'"

But the snake said to the woman, "You will not die. God knows that if you eat the fruit from that tree, you will learn about good and evil. Then you will be like God!"

The woman saw that the tree was beautiful. She saw that its fruit was good to eat and that it would make her wise. So she took some of its fruit and ate it. She also gave some of the fruit to her husband who was with her, and he ate it.

choice

Sweet Dreams Devotion

Do you ever find it hard to pay attention to what your mom or dad tells you? You're kind of listening, but your mind wanders off. Well, Adam and Eve weren't paying attention either, and it led them into huge trouble. God had told them exactly what they needed to do to stay happy in the beautiful garden of Eden. But, in the form of a snake, Satan confused Eve. He tricked her into thinking that God's way was not the best. He made her think that God was keeping something good away from Adam and Eve. So she disobeyed God and ate from the very tree that

Dear Jesus, thank you for helping me become God's friend. Help me to fight Satan's lies and **listen** only to you and your **Word**.

Praise

God said not to. Then Adam did the same thing. They knew right away it was a mistake. They knew they had broken their relationship with God, and it made them very sad.

Are you ever tempted to disobey God? Does it seem like sin is more fun? Don't be tricked! We are never happy apart from God. His ways are always best. Ask God now to help you always obey him.

Noah Builds a Boat

T his is the family history of Noah. Noah was a good man. He was the most innocent man of his time. He walked with God. Noah had three sons: Shem, Ham and Japheth.

People on earth did what God said was evil. Violence was everywhere. And God saw this evil. All people on the earth did only evil. So God said to Noah, "People have made the earth full of violence. So I will destroy all people from the earth. Build a boat of cypress wood for yourself. Make rooms in it and cover it inside and outside with tar. This is how big I want you to build the boat: 450 feet long, 75 feet wide and 45 feet high…. I will bring a flood of water on the earth. I will destroy all living things that live under the sky. This includes everything that has the breath of life. Everything on the earth will die. But I will make an agreement with you. You, your sons, your wife and your sons' wives will all go into the boat."…

Noah did everything that God commanded him.

Sweet Dreams Devotion

Have you ever been embarrassed because you didn't look or act like everyone else? Perhaps your hair won't stay flat, or you laugh really loudly and it makes people stare at you. How does that make you feel?

Noah probably felt a little funny, too. He was different from everyone around him. No one in his town believed in God. They had also never seen rain before. Can you imagine that! But God told Noah he needed to build a boat to save his family from the coming flood. Noah could have told God no, but he didn't.

Noah cared more about what God thought than what anyone else thought.

Noah and his family were the only people on earth who survived the worldwide flood.

Sometimes it's hard to do what's right. Other people might not understand why we do our best to obey God and His Word. They may even make fun of us. But it's never foolish to obey God. We experience the biggest blessings when we stick with him!

PROMISE:

God put a **RAINBOW** in the sky as a promise. He would never flood the earth that way again!

The Great Flood

hen the Lord said to Noah, "I have seen that you are the best man among the people of this time. So you and your family go into the boat. Take with you seven pairs, each male with its female, of every kind of clean animal. And take one pair, each male with its female, of every kind of un-clean animal. Take seven pairs of all the birds of the sky, each male with its fe-male. This will allow all these animals to continue living on the earth after the flood. Seven days from now I will send rain on the earth. It will rain 40 days and 40 nights. I will destroy from the earth every living thing that I made."

Noah did everything that the Lord commanded him.

Noah was 600 years old when the flood came. He and his wife and his sons and their wives went into the boat. They went in to escape the waters of the flood. The clean animals, the unclean animals, the birds and everything that crawls on the ground came to Noah. They went into the boat in groups of two, male and female. This was just as God had commanded Noah. Seven days later the flood started.

promise

Sweet Dreams Devotion

Have you ever been to the zoo? What was it like? How did it smell? It may have needed some Princess perfume!

Now imagine having all those animals live inside your house! Noah and his family lived with all kinds of animals inside the boat for almost a year! How did he ever feed and clean so many creatures? Maybe we can ask him that in heaven one day. But for now, we can be thankful for Noah's obedience and God's special way of saving him. When the flood waters went down, the boat rested on top of a mountain. Noah and his family and all the animals finally got off their floating zoo and gave thanks to God for his goodness to them.

Does your house ever seem like a zoo? It can be hard getting along with your brothers and sisters sometimes. But remember that God sees. Trust him to take care of you—even when life seems a little crazy.

prayer

Dear God, thank you for taking care of me. Help me to be kind to my family as we live together under your care.

The Tower of Babel

 t this time the whole world spoke one language. Everyone used the same words. As people moved from the East, they found a plain in the land of Babylonia. They settled there to live.

They said to each other, "Let's make bricks and bake them to make them hard." So they used bricks instead of stones, and tar instead of mortar. Then they said to each other, "Let's build for ourselves a city and a tower. And let's make the top of the tower reach high into the sky. We will become famous. If we do this, we will not be scattered over all the earth."

22

The Lord came down to see the city and the tower that the people had built. The Lord said, "Now, these people are united. They all speak the same language. This is only the beginning of what they will do. They will be able to do anything they want. Come, let us go down and confuse their language. Then they will not be able to understand each other."

So the Lord scattered them from there over all the earth. And they stopped building the city. That is where the Lord confused the language of the whole world. So the place is called Babel. So the Lord caused them to spread out from there over all the whole world.

Sweet Dreams Devotion

Have you ever built a tower with blocks? What eventually happens if you build it too tall? Yes, that's right; the whole thing comes tumbling down. The men from Bible times ran into the same problem, only they were building their tower with real bricks. They had all gotten together and decided to build something so tall it would reach God. They were really just saying they wanted to be more powerful than God.

It was not a good idea. God stopped that foolish plan. He made them speak in different languages so they couldn't understand each other anymore. They couldn't work together to build the tower, so they all separated to go be with people they could understand.

Trying to live life our own way is about as silly as building a tower to reach heaven. Both efforts fail. We need to love and serve God instead. He alone helps us understand him and each other.

PROMISE:

God says that he is
the best builder there is.
Ask God today
to help you **BUILD** a good life
by obeying his Word!

Abram & Sarai

Then the Lord said to Abram, "Leave your country, your relatives and your father's family. Go to the land I will show you.

I will make you a great nation, and I will bless you. I will make you famous. And you will be a blessing to others.

I will bless those who bless you. I will place a curse on those who harm you. And all the people on earth will be blessed through you."

So Abram left Haran as the Lord had told him. And Lot went with him. At this time Abram was 75 years old.

Abram took his wife Sarai, his nephew Lot and everything they owned. They took all the servants they had gotten in Haran. They set out from Haran, planning to go to the land of Canaan. In time they arrived there.

Abram traveled through that land. He went as far as the great tree of Moreh at Shechem. The Canaanites were living in the land at that time. The Lord appeared to Abram. The Lord said, "I will give this land to your descendants." So Abram built an altar there to the Lord, who had appeared to him.

blessing

Sweet Dreams Devotion

Have you had a good day, Princess? Look around your room. What makes your room special? What do you love most about where you live? Your neighborhood friends? Your school? What would you do if God suddenly appeared to your mom or dad and told your family to move to a new place? Would you be scared? Sad? Excited?

Abram probably felt everything all at once. But he knew that if he followed God's lead, he would end up in the best place possible. God rewarded Abram's faith and blessed him in a big way. He gave him land and a huge family!

It's not always easy to follow God. It can even seem scary to do something new. Like Abram, we need to trust God! Big blessings lie just around the corner.

Promise

God promises to never leave you or take his eyes off you!

Sarah Laughs

GENESIS 18:1-2, 9-16

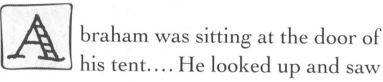braham was sitting at the door of his tent.... He looked up and saw three men standing near him....

The men asked Abraham, "Where is your wife Sarah?"

"There, in the tent," said Abraham.

Then the Lord said, "I will certainly return to you about this time a year from now. At that time your wife Sarah will have a son."

Sarah was listening at the entrance of the tent which was behind him. Abraham and Sarah were very old. Sarah was past the age when women normally have children. So she laughed to herself, "My husband and I are too old to have a baby."

Then the Lord said to Abraham, "Why did Sarah laugh? Why did she say, 'I am too old to have a baby'? Is anything too hard for the Lord? No! I will return to you at the right time a year from now. And Sarah will have a son."

Sarah was afraid. So she lied and said, "I didn't laugh."

But the Lord said, "No. You did laugh."

Then the men got up to leave and started out toward Sodom. Abraham walked along with them a short time to send them on their way.

Sweet Dreams Devotion

If your brother or sister told you they could capture the moon with a rope, would you laugh? It's hard not to. Roping the moon is about as impossible as an old woman having a baby...which is why Sarah couldn't keep the giggles inside.

Sarah was old—older than your grandmother or possibly even your great-grandmother. She was too old to have a baby, and she knew it. But she should have known that anything is possible with God. Isn't it wonderful to be his Princess!

God promised her she would have a baby in her old age. At first, she laughed. But God didn't. He was serious! At around age 100, Abraham and Sarah had a baby boy and named him Isaac. No doubt, Sarah laughed again when Isaac was born — but that time out of joy over God's amazing power! And then I'm sure she took a nap.

Praise

Dear God, you created the world and all that is in it. Nothing is too difficult for you!

Rebekah

GENESIS 24:15-21,
23-27

 Rebekah was carrying her water jar on her shoulder.... She went down to the spring and filled her jar. Then she came back up. [Abraham's] servant ran to her and said, "Please give me a little water from your jar."

Rebekah said, "Drink, sir." She quickly lowered the jar from her shoulder and gave him a drink. After he finished drinking, Rebekah said, "I will also pour some water for your camels." So she quickly poured all the water from her jar into the drinking trough for the camels. Then she kept running to the well until she had given all the camels enough to drink.

The servant quietly watched her. He wanted to be sure the Lord had made his trip successful.... The servant asked, "Who is your father? Is there a place in his house for me and my men to spend the night?"

Rebekah answered, "My father is Bethuel. He is the son of Milcah and Nahor." Then she said, "And, yes, we have straw for your camels. We have a place for you to spend the night."

The servant bowed and worshiped the Lord. He said, "Blessed is the Lord, the God of my master Abraham. The Lord has been kind and truthful to him. He has led me to my master's relatives."

helpful

Sweet Dreams Devotion

Rebekah didn't know Abraham's servant was watching her. She just saw some thirsty camels and wanted to help. So she took her own watering jar and gave them all a drink. She had no idea that she would get such a giant blessing for her kindness. By being such a sweet servant, she proved that she was the one God had chosen to marry Isaac.

You can be helpful like Rebekah too. It might be hard to find a camel that needs water, but perhaps your dog or cat or hamster might like some. You could help your mom with the dishes, or you can let your little brother or sister have a turn first at a favorite family game. You can share your candy with your friends. God gives us little chances every day to serve him. Even the smallest act of kindness brings God glory.

Prayer

Dear Lord, help me to notice when I can be of help. Give me the strength to always do what is right.

Esau & Jacob

Isaac's wife could not have children. So Isaac prayed to the Lord for her. The Lord heard Isaac's prayer, and Rebekah became pregnant.

While she was pregnant, the babies struggled inside her. She asked, "Why is this happening to me?" Then she went to get an answer from the Lord.

The Lord said to her, "Two nations are in your body. Two groups of people will be taken from you. One group will be stronger than the other. The older will serve the younger."

And when the time came, Rebekah gave birth to twins. The first baby was born red. His skin was like a hairy robe. So he was named Esau. When the second baby was born, he was holding on to Esau's heel. So that baby was named Jacob. Isaac was 60 years old when they were born.

divided

Sweet Dreams Devotion

As you learn from this story, God's Princesses have problems too. Rebekah had a problem that made her very sad. She knew she wanted a family, but she just couldn't seem to have a baby. Her husband, Isaac, went to the one who could fix the problem. Isaac prayed to God.

Guess what God did? That's right! He answered Isaac's prayer. In fact, God gave them two babies at the same time! They moved around so much inside Rebekah that she needed help again. This time she went to God on her own and asked for wisdom. God also answered her prayer.

Do you ever need help? Do you ever feel stuck in a situation and you just don't know what to do or where to turn? As God's Princess, Rebekah turned to the King, her Father God. Remember that God has all power and he loves you. Go to him with all of your needs. He will answer your prayers in a way that is best for you too.

Praise

God, I praise you because you can do all things. You listen to me when I pray, and I can trust you to do what is best!

Joseph's Jealous Brothers

Joseph was born when his father Israel, also called Jacob, was old. So Israel loved Joseph more than his other sons. He made Joseph a special robe with long sleeves.... Joseph's brothers saw that their father loved Joseph more than he loved them. So they hated their brother and could not speak to him politely.

Jacob said to Joseph, "Go to Shechem. Your brothers are there herding the sheep."

Joseph answered, "I will go."

His father said, "Go and see if your brothers and the sheep are all right. Then come back and tell me."...

When Joseph came to Shechem, a man found him wandering in the field. He asked Joseph, "What are you looking for?"

Joseph answered, "I am looking for my brothers. Can you tell me where they are herding the sheep?"

The man said, "They have already gone. I heard them say they were going to Dothan." So Joseph went to look for his brothers and found them in Dothan.

Joseph's brothers saw him coming from far away. Before he reached them, they made a plan to kill him. They said to each other, "Here comes that dreamer. Let's kill him and throw his body into one of the wells. We can tell our father that a wild animal killed him. Then we will see what will become of his dreams."

Sweet Dreams Devotion

This is kind of a sad story, don't you think? Joseph's brothers didn't like Joseph very much. Joseph proudly wore a colorful coat that his father had given only to him, and I'm sure that made his brothers jealous. They wanted their father to show that he loved them as much as he loved Joseph.

Joseph's father sinned by loving one child more than the others. His sin led his other sons to sin badly too. They wanted to kill Joseph and planned a way to do it. Have you ever had a new dress or a Princess crown and you wanted to show your friends? It's good

Dear Lord, please **search** my heart and see if any sin is hiding in it. Show me what is right and **good**, and help me to follow it.

Prayer

to be able to share our happiness, but not when we want the other person to feel badly that they don't have one.

Joseph's father and brothers remind us of how dangerous sin can be in our lives. Our own bad thoughts and actions hurt others—and ourselves. When we see sin in our hearts, the first thing a Princess should do is tell God about it right away. Ask for forgiveness, and ask him for strength to live God's way.

Joseph Sold into Slavery

GENESIS 37:21-28

Reuben heard their plan and saved Joseph. He said, "Let's not kill him. Don't spill any blood. Throw him into this well here in the desert. But don't hurt him!" Reuben planned to save Joseph later and send him back to his father. So when Joseph came to his brothers, they pulled off his robe with long sleeves. Then they threw him into the well. It was empty. There was no water in it.

While Joseph was in the well, the brothers sat down to eat. When they looked up, they saw a group of Ishma-elites. They were traveling from Gilead

46

to Egypt. Their camels were carrying spices, balm and myrrh.

Then Judah said to his brothers, "What will we gain if we kill our brother and hide his death? Let's sell him to these Ishmaelites. Then we will not be guilty of killing our own brother. After all, he is our brother, our own flesh and blood." And the other brothers agreed. So when the Midianite traders came by, the brothers took Joseph out of the well. They sold him to the Ishmaelites for eight ounces of silver. And the Ishmael-ites took him to Egypt.

Sweet Dreams Devotion

Do you ever wish you could trade your brother or sister in for a new one? Joseph's brothers sure did. Only they had the chance to really do it. In just a few moments of really bad thinking, the brothers sold Joseph as a slave to some Egyptians passing by. Can you imagine that they would do such a mean thing?

Poor Joseph! What was he going to do now? He couldn't do anything at all except trust that God would somehow make things right again.

After Joseph left, his father cried and cried. Do you think his brothers felt badly for what they did? Do you think they missed him, or wished they hadn't made their father so sad by taking Joseph away?

Even though our family members may bother us sometimes, we need to always remember that each person is a blessing, and if they went away we would really miss them. Take time now to thank God for the people in your family, and tell them why you are glad they are in your life.

PRAYER:

Dear God, help me to **LOVE** my family members well and to be thankful for them. Show me ways I can **SERVE** and love them better.

Joseph Explains Dreams

GENESIS 40:5-9, 12-13, 16, 18

One night both the king's officer who served him wine and the baker had a dream. Each had his own dream with its own meaning. When Joseph came to them the next morning, he saw they were worried. Joseph asked the king's officers who were with him, "Why do you look so unhappy today?"

The two men answered, "We both had dreams last night. But no one can explain the meaning of them to us."

Joseph said to them, "God is the only One who can explain the meaning of dreams. So tell me your dreams."

So the man who served wine to the king told Joseph his dream....

Then Joseph said, "I will explain the dream to you. The three branches stand for three days. Before the end of three days the king will free you. He will allow you to return to your work. You will serve the king his wine just as you did before....

The baker saw that Joseph's explanation of the dream was good. So he said to Joseph, "I also had a dream."...

Joseph answered, "I will tell you what the dream means. The three baskets stand for three days. Before the end of three days, the king will cut off your head! He will hang your body on a pole. And the birds will eat your flesh."

Sweet Dreams Devotion

What's the craziest dream you've ever had? Have you ever dreamed that you had your own castle and servants and a wardrobe full of perfect, pink Princess dresses? Dreams can be a lot of fun.

Joseph had lots of dreams too. God even gave Joseph the ability to tell other people what their dreams meant. When Joseph was in prison, two of the other prisoners had very strange dreams. They were bothered by them, so they asked Joseph to help them understand the dreams.

Joseph told them that he couldn't tell them the meaning of their dreams without God's help. So God explained the dreams to Joseph, and Joseph told the men. The message in both dreams came true just a few days later.

Do you have a special gift or talent? Perhaps you can sing or you love to help other people. God says that every good thing we have comes from him. Remember to give God the credit whenever you do something great!

praise

God, you are so good!
I praise you because you make me able to do great things.

From Prison to Palace

GENESIS 41:14-16, 32-33, 37-40

The king called for Joseph. The guards quickly brought him out of the prison. He shaved, put on clean clothes and went before the king.

The king said to Joseph, "I have had a dream. But no one can explain its meaning to me. I have heard that you can explain a dream when someone tells it to you."

Joseph answered the king, "I am not able to explain the meaning of dreams. God will do this for the king."…

"You had two dreams which mean the same thing. This shows that God has

firmly decided that this will happen.
And he will make it happen soon.

"So let the king choose
a man who is very wise
and understanding. Let
the king set him over the
land of Egypt...."

This seemed like a very good
idea to the king. All his officers agreed.
And the king asked them, "Can we find
a better man than Joseph to take this
job? God's spirit is truly in him!"

So the king said to Joseph, "God has
shown you all this. There is no one as
wise and understanding as you are.
I will put you in charge of my palace.
All the people will obey your orders.
Only I will be greater than you."

Sweet Dreams Devotion

Joseph had been in prison a long time, even though he didn't do anything wrong. Can you imagine how hard that must have been? After many years Pharaoh, which is the Egyptian name for king, had a dream he didn't understand. He remembered that Joseph could explain dreams, so he had him released from prison to help him. At last Joseph was free, and he was made ruler over Egypt, second only to Pharaoh.

Why did God allow Joseph's life to be so hard at first? We know now from the rest of the story that God was training

Joseph, but Joseph didn't know that during those long years in prison. God knew he had great plans for Joseph to rescue his own family from starvation. But he needed to strengthen Joseph's faith and character first.

Sometimes God has to train us too. You may get disciplined by your mom or dad and at times it can feel hard or unfair, but they do it because they love you. Discipline can help you grow up to be a stronger woman of God.

PROMISE:

Discipline will produce the kind of life that honors God if we **LEARN** by it!

The Israelites Become Slaves

EXODUS 1:8-11, 14-17

A new king began to rule Egypt. He did not know who Joseph was. This king said to his people, "Look! The people of Israel are too many! And they are too strong for us to handle! We must make plans against them. If we don't, the number of their people will grow even more. Then if there is a war, they might join our enemies. Then they could fight us and escape from the country!"

58

So the Egyptians made life hard for the people of Israel. They put slave masters over the Israelites.... They forced the Israelites to work very hard making bricks and mortar. They also forced them to do all kinds of hard work in the fields. The Egyptians were not merciful to them in all their hard work.

There were two Hebrew nurses named Shiphrah and Puah. These nurses helped the Israelite women give birth to their babies. The king of Egypt said to the nurses, "When you are helping the Hebrew women give birth to their babies, watch! If the baby is a girl, let the baby live. But if it is a boy, kill it!" But the nurses feared God. So they did not do as the king told them. They let all the boy babies live.

Sweet Dreams Devotion

Joseph and his brothers and their families stayed in Egypt until they died. Their children and grandchildren grew and had more and more children until there were more Israelites (Abraham's family) than there were Egyptians! Imagine how much fun it would be at all those birthday parties!

The Egyptians got scared that the Israelites would try to take over their land. They said that any baby boys that were born would have to be killed. There are some very bad people in the world, which makes it so wonderful to be watched over by God our Father and by those who love him. The ladies who helped the Israelite women have their babies didn't listen to the Egyptians. They listened to God instead. They helped the new babies escape death, and God blessed them for it.

No matter what anyone else says or believes, we must do what God says is right. It's not always easy to follow God, but his way brings bigger blessings than we can even imagine.

Prayer

Dear Lord, teach me your ways.
Help me to follow you
and not the people around me
who don't know you.

Baby Moses and His Sister

The king commanded all his people: "Every time a boy is born to the Hebrews, you must throw him into the Nile River. But let all the girl babies live."

There was a man from the family of Levi. He married a woman who was also from the family of Levi. She became pregnant and gave birth to a son. She saw how wonderful the baby was, and she hid him for three months. But after three months, she was not able to hide the baby any longer. So she got a basket made of reeds and covered it with tar so that it would float. She put the baby in the basket. Then she put the basket among the tall grass at the edge of the Nile River. The baby's sister stood a short distance away. She wanted to see what would happen to him.

Then the daughter of the king of Egypt came to the river.... She saw the basket in the tall grass. So she sent her slave girl to get it. The king's daughter opened the basket and saw the baby boy. He was crying, and she felt sorry for him. She said, "This is one of the Hebrew babies."

Then the baby's sister asked the king's daughter, "Would you like me to find a Hebrew woman to nurse the baby for you?"

The king's daughter said, "Yes, please." So the girl went and got the baby's own mother.

Sweet Dreams Devotion

Do you ever feel like you're too young to really help? You're not! God uses even young people to help build his kingdom! I'm sure that Miriam felt like there wasn't much she could do to change the world, but in God's hands every little Princess is powerful.

She was the older sister of baby Moses. She watched over him carefully as her mom placed him in the floating basket. She was standing nearby when Pharaoh's daughter discovered him in the tall grass. Quickly, Miriam took action. She offered to find an Israelite woman to help her raise the boy.

God, even though I am small, you promise to be the **strength** I need to do your mighty work!

Praise

When Pharaoh's daughter agreed, Miriam got their own mom! Yeah, Mom! Yeah, Miriam!

Miriam's action saved her little brother's life. Her brother would grow up to rescue all the Israelites from the Egyptians.

Remember that God uses even small acts of obedience to make really great things happen. Ask God to help you be ready for action when the time comes!

God Calls Moses

EXODUS 3:2-7, 10-12

The angel of the Lord appeared to Moses in flames of fire coming out of a bush. Moses saw that the bush was on fire, but it was not burning up. So Moses said, "I will go closer to this strange thing. How can a bush continue burning without burning up?"

The Lord saw Moses was coming to look at the bush. So God called to him from the bush, "Moses, Moses!"

And Moses said, "Here I am."

Then God said, "Do not come any closer. Take off your sandals. You are standing on holy ground. I am the God of your ancestors. I am the God of Abraham, the God of Isaac and the God of Jacob." Moses covered his face because he was afraid to look at God.

The Lord said, "I have seen the troubles my people have suffered in Egypt. And I have heard their cries when the Egyptian slave masters hurt them…. So now I am sending you to the king of Egypt. Go! Bring my people, the Israelites, out of Egypt!"

But Moses said to God, "I am not a great man! Why should I be the one to go to the king and lead the Israelites out of Egypt?"

God said, "I will be with you. This will be the proof that I am sending you: You will lead the people out of Egypt. Then all of you will worship me on this mountain."

Sweet Dreams Devotion

God had saved Moses as a baby in the floating basket. He had rescued Moses from Pharaoh after Moses had protected some Israelite slaves. Now God was asking Moses to help him save his people from the Egyptians, and that was scary! Don't you think it's scary to do something you've never done before?

Moses had seen God working in his life all along. But Moses didn't like God's idea for saving Israel. "I'm not smart enough. I don't speak well enough. I'm not good enough," Moses said to God. So God told Moses what he wants all of his people to know. When God asks us to do something, he gives us the power to do it. We can obey because God will take care of all the details. We should say yes to God when he asks us to obey him. When we do, we get to see God's miracles with our own eyes. That is very exciting stuff!

PRAYER:

Lord, help me to **BELIEVE**
that you can do anything
you want to do through me.
I want to be your servant. Please
give me a willing and believing **HEART**.

Miracles in Egypt

EXODUS 7:1-5; 8:1-6

The Lord said to Moses, "I have made you like God to the king of Egypt. And your brother Aaron will be like a prophet for you. Tell Aaron your brother everything that I command you. Then let him tell the king of Egypt to let the Israelites leave his country. But I will make the king stubborn. Then I will do many miracles in Egypt. But he will still refuse to listen. So then I will punish Egypt terribly. And I will lead my divisions, my people the Israelites, out of that land.... Then they will know I am the Lord."...

The Lord told Moses, "Go to the king of Egypt and tell him, 'This is what the Lord says: Let my people go to worship me. If you refuse, then I will punish Egypt with frogs. The Nile River will be filled with frogs. They will come from the river and enter your palace. They will be in your bedroom and your bed.... They will enter your ovens and your baking pans. The frogs will jump up all over you, your people and your officers.'"

Then the Lord said to Moses, "Tell Aaron to hold his walking stick in his hand over the rivers, canals and ponds...."

So Aaron held his hand over all the waters of Egypt. The frogs came up out of the water and covered the land of Egypt.

Sweet Dreams Devotion

It started with Moses' staff becoming a snake. Pharaoh wasn't impressed. Next came the river of blood. Still Pharaoh didn't care. Then God sent the frogs, the gnats, and the flies. Doesn't that sound yucky—frogs and flies all over your peanut butter and jelly sandwich! Pharaoh would change, but then turn back again to his old, disobedient ways. Then came the animal sickness, the awful boils, the hail, the hungry locusts, and the scary darkness. Nothing seemed to speak to Pharaoh's very hard heart.

Then God killed the firstborn son from every Egyptian family, including Pharaoh's. At last Pharaoh listened. God was in control, not Pharaoh. He saw that every breath is in God's hands. So at last, he let God's people go.

When God tells us to do something, it really makes more sense to listen the first time. Perhaps you know that God wants you to stop a bad habit, but it's so hard. Ask God to give you the strength to say yes to him!

prayer

Lord, thank you that you love me. Please help me say yes to you the first time.

A Dry Path to Freedom

EXODUS 14:8-10, 13-16, 21-22

The Lord made the king of Egypt stubborn. So he chased the Israelites, who were leaving victoriously. The king of Egypt came with his horses, chariot drivers and army. And they chased the Israelites....

The Israelites saw the king and his army coming after them. They were very frightened and cried to the Lord for help....

But Moses said, "Don't be afraid! Stand still and see the Lord save you today. You will never see these Egyptians again after today. You will only need to remain calm. The Lord will fight for you."

Then the Lord said to Moses, "Why are you crying out to me? Command the people of Israel to start moving. Raise your walking stick and hold it over the sea. The sea will split. Then the people can cross the sea on dry land...."

Moses held his hand over the sea. All that night the Lord drove back the sea with a strong east wind. And so he made the sea become dry ground. The water was split. And the Israelites went through the sea on dry land. A wall of water was on both sides.

Sweet Dreams Devotion

Do you ever have a hard time remembering that God is always with you, even when something difficult happens? You are not alone. God's people had a very short memory too. They had just seen God perform eleven amazing miracles. It was quite clear that God was with them. Not only did they get to leave Egypt, but they also got to take a lot of the Egyptian's gold with them when they left. It was as if they had their very own Princess jewels.

But then they had a new problem. Egyptian soldiers were coming after them, and a sea of water blocked the path in front of them. So what did they do? They complained to Moses! They became afraid and forgot the power of God.

It's a good thing God loves us even when we're foolish. He showed his mighty power to Israel again. He simply split the water in half and made a dry path for them to cross to safety.

We need to learn Israel's lesson. God never leaves us. We don't have to be afraid. We should always trust God to come to our rescue because he will!

PRAISE:

Thank you, God,
     for being **PATIENT** with me
when I forget that you are always there
     to help me when I **CALL** on you.

Bread from Heaven

The whole Israelite community grumbled to Moses and Aaron in the desert. The Israelites said to them, "It would have been better if the Lord had killed us in the land of Egypt. There we had meat to eat. We had all the food we wanted. But you have brought us into this desert. You will starve us to death here."

Then the Lord said to Moses, "I will cause food to fall like rain from the sky. This food will be for all of you. Every day the people must go out and gather what they need for that day. I will do this to see if the people will do what I teach them. On the sixth day of each week, they are to gather twice as much as they gather on other days. Then they are to prepare it."

So Moses and Aaron said to all the Israelites: "This evening you will know that the Lord is the one who brought you out of Egypt. Tomorrow morning you will see the greatness of the Lord. He has heard you grumble against him. We are nothing. You are not grumbling against us, but against the Lord."

Sweet Dreams Devotion

Shhhh! Do you hear that grumbling sound? Perhaps it's your mom or dad's tummy? It might be coming from the hungry Israelite tummies? No! The noise you heard was Israel complaining to God. They got scared again and wondered where they were going to find food to eat. Instead of asking nicely, they acted like spoiled little babies who wanted their own way. They forgot that God had a plan, and his plan was for their good.

God provided sweet flakes of bread called manna that came from heaven. Each day the people were to gather just what they needed. If they tried to get too much, it would go bad. They got tired of manna and started telling God what they thought he should do.

God wanted the Israelites and us to know that he loves to take care of us. We don't need to complain or worry about what we eat or wear because God will provide all we need. We also don't need to be greedy and take more than we need. We share with others because we know God takes care of us.

Prayer

Lord, please forgive me when I am not grateful for everything you provide for me every single day. Help me not to take your kindness for granted.

Ten Commandments

EXODUS 20:1-5, 7-10, 12-17

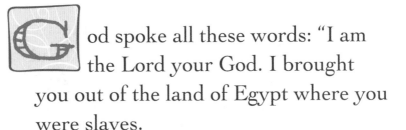

God spoke all these words: "I am the Lord your God. I brought you out of the land of Egypt where you were slaves.

"You must not have any other gods except me.

"You must not make for yourselves any idols…. You must not worship or serve any idol. This is because I, the Lord your God, am a jealous God….

"You must not use the name of the Lord your God thoughtlessly. The Lord will punish anyone who is guilty and misuses his name.

"Remember to keep the Sabbath as a holy day. You may work and get everything done during six days each week. But the seventh day is a day of rest to honor the Lord your God....

"Honor your father and your mother. Then you will live a long time in the land....

"You must not murder anyone.

"You must not be guilty of adultery.

"You must not steal.

"You must not tell lies about your neighbor in court....

"You must not want to take anything that belongs to your neighbor."

Obey

What do you think would happen if we didn't have rules? What would your house be like? The dog might bury his favorite bone in your bed, or your brother might use your extra-special, pink Princess toothbrush. What would happen on the streets if people drove however they wanted to? That could get really messy.

All people need rules in order to live well together and to keep everyone safe. We may

not always like them, but they are for our own good.

God also has a list of rules we call the Ten Commandments. They are the ten ways God instructs us to love him and others. God gave the commandments to the Hebrews because they needed to know how they were supposed to behave since they belonged to God. They weren't like any other nation. They were God's special people.

We are God's special people too. God's rules are still important today. They help us understand who God is and how we should act as his Princesses.

The Golden Calf

EXODUS 32:1-4, 7-8

he people saw that a long time had passed. And Moses had not come down from the mountain. So they gathered around Aaron. They said to him, "Moses led us out of Egypt. But we don't know what has happened to him. So make us gods who will lead us."

Aaron said to the people, "Take off the gold earrings that your wives, sons and daughters are wearing. Bring them to me." So all the people took their gold earrings and brought them to Aaron. Aaron took the gold from the people. Then he melted it and made a statue of a calf. He finished it with a tool. Then the people said, "Israel! These are your gods who brought you out of the land of Egypt!"...

And the Lord said to Moses, "Go down from this mountain. Your people, the people you brought out of the land of Egypt, have done a terrible sin. They have quickly turned away from the things I commanded them to do. They have made for themselves a calf of melted gold. They have worshiped that calf and offered sacrifices to it."

idols

Sweet Dreams Devotion

Have you ever seen a cow? What do they sound like? What do they provide for us that we use almost every day?

The Israelites thought a golden cow would make a really good idol to worship instead of the true and living God. Do you think that was a good idea? Just imagine how silly it would be to worship a dog or the neighbor's cat!

God says that we should never worship anything or anyone except him. When Moses returned from the mountain and saw what the people had made while he was gone, he got very angry. God was angry too. Many people died because of their great sin.

We may think it is very silly that Israel made a golden calf and worshiped it. But whenever we make someone or something in our lives more important than God, we can be making idols too. Ask God to help you keep your heart set only on him.

PRAYER:

Father, help me to see if anything
in my life is taking your place.
I don't want to love my toys,
or my clothes, or even my friends
more than I love **YOU**.

Pillar and Cloud of Fire

On the day the Holy Tent was set up, a cloud covered it. (The Holy Tent was also called the Tent of the Agreement.) From dusk until dawn the cloud above the Tent looked like fire. The cloud stayed above the Tent. At night it looked like fire. When the cloud moved from its place over the Tent, the Israelites moved. Wherever the cloud stopped, the Israelites camped. So the Israelites moved at the Lord's command. And they camped at his command. While the cloud stayed over the Tent, they stayed in place. Sometimes the cloud stayed over the

Tent for a long time. The Israelites obeyed the Lord and did not move. Sometimes the cloud was over it only a few days. At the Lord's command the people camped. And at his command they moved. Sometimes the cloud stayed only from dusk until dawn. When the cloud lifted the next morning, the people moved. When the cloud lifted, day or night, the people moved. The cloud might stay over the Tent for two days, a month or a year. As long as it stayed, the people would camp. But when the cloud lifted, they moved. At the Lord's command the people camped. And at his command they moved. They obeyed the Lord's order that he commanded through Moses.

Sweet Dreams Devotion

If your parents said they were going to take you to a wonderful place, like the beach or a fun theme park, would you be excited? What if you had to wait days or weeks before you got to have the special treat they promised? It's so hard to wait!

God's people had to learn to wait for God's blessing. They knew he had promised them a wonderful land, but they didn't know where it was. They had to follow God's lead. God decided to take the shape of a cloud during the day and a fire at night. As long as he stayed over the Tent, the people stayed. When God moved, the people moved. They followed God wherever he went because they knew God would keep his promise.

What are some ways God might lead you? From the Bible, God gives us lots of help to know how to live. God also speaks to us through our Sunday school teachers and our families. God loves to lead his precious Princesses.

prayer

Dear Jesus, help me to recognize all the ways that you want to lead me, and teach me how to follow you.

Balaam's Donkey

NUMBERS 22:22-28, 31

Balaam ... put a saddle on his donkey. Then he went with the Moabite leaders. But God became angry because Balaam went. So the angel of the Lord stood in the road to stop Balaam.... The donkey saw the angel of the Lord standing in the road. The angel had a sword in his hand. So the donkey left the road and went into the field. Balaam hit the donkey to force her back on the road.

Later, the angel of the Lord stood on a narrow path between two vineyards. There were walls on both sides. Again the donkey saw the angel of the Lord.

So the donkey walked close to one wall. This crushed Balaam's foot against the wall. So he hit her again.

The angel of the Lord went ahead again. The angel stood at a narrow place. It was too narrow to turn left or right. The donkey saw the angel of the Lord. So she lay down under Balaam. Balaam was very angry and hit her with his stick. Then the Lord made the donkey talk. She said to Balaam, "What have I done to make you hit me three times?"…

Then the Lord let Balaam see the angel. The angel of the Lord was standing in the road with his sword drawn. Then Balaam bowed facedown on the ground.

listen

Sweet Dreams Devotion

Do you like animals? What's your very favorite one? Wouldn't it be fun if our pets could really talk to us? What if, while you were playing, one of them spoke out loud? What would you think?

Balaam got to find out. One day Balaam was riding a donkey, headed to a bad place. Balaam wanted to disobey God, but the donkey he was riding did not. God had put an invisible angel with a flaming sword right in the middle of their path. The donkey could see him and did everything she could to stop. Balaam just kept hitting the donkey.

So God made the donkey speak. She let Balaam know that he was doing a bad thing. Then God showed Balaam the hidden angel, and Balaam told God he was sorry.

Why would we ever want to go against God? He loves us and wants the best for us!

P.S. It wouldn't be a good idea to disobey God just to see if your cat will speak. I think this was just for Balaam!

PROMISE:

God says that we may make plans, but he directs our **STEPS**!

Wall of Jericho

The Lord spoke to Joshua. He said, "Look, I have given you Jericho, its king and all its fighting men. March around the city with your army one time every day. Do this for six days. Have seven priests carry trumpets made from horns of male sheep. Tell them to march in front of the Holy Box. On the seventh day march around the city seven times. On that day tell the priests to blow the trumpets as they march. They will make one long blast on the trumpets. When you hear that sound, have all the people give a loud shout. Then the walls of the city will fall. And the people will go straight into the city."…

So…they marched around the city one time. Then they went back to camp. They did this every day for six days.

On the seventh day they got up at dawn. They marched around the city seven times…. The seventh time around the priests blew their trumpets. Then Joshua gave the command: "Now, shout! The Lord has given you this city!…

When the priests blew the trumpets, the people shouted. At the sound of the trumpets and the people's shout, the walls fell. And everyone ran straight into the city. So the Israelites defeated that city.

Sweet Dreams Devotion

Have you ever seen a parade? Was it fun to watch the people walking by? Why don't you have a Princess parade with your friends? You could ask your mom to help you put it all together, with pink feather boas and sparkly tiaras.

The people of Jericho got to watch a parade of sorts, but it was not a fun kind for them. God had told his people to march around Jericho's city wall once each day. Then on the seventh day, they marched around it seven times. They blew trumpets and everyone yelled as loud as boys do at recess. Then the parade was over. Jericho's city

God, I praise you because your ways
are **smarter** and better than mine.
I choose to **follow** you!

Praise

walls crumbled to the ground, and the
Israelites rushed in to take over the city.

God doesn't often work the way we
think he will. But God's plan always
works better than we can imagine. Ask
him to help you understand the plan
he gives us in the Bible. Follow God—
no matter how different
his way seems.

Deborah

JUDGES 4:4, 6-9

There was a prophetess named Deborah. She was the wife of Lappidoth. She was judge of Israel at that time....

Deborah sent a message to a man named Barak.... Deborah said to Barak, "The Lord, the God of Israel, commands you: 'Go and gather 10,000 men of Naphtali and Zebulun. Lead them to Mount Tabor. I will make Sisera, the commander of Jabin's army, come to you. Sisera, his chariots and his army will meet you at the Kishon River. I will help you to defeat Sisera there.'"

Then Barak said to Deborah, "I will go if you will go with me. But if you will not go with me, I won't go."

"Of course I will go with you," Deborah answered. "But you will not get credit for the victory. The Lord will let a woman defeat Sisera."

victory

Sweet Dreams Devotion

Barak had a problem. He was a soldier, and God had given him a tough job to do. But he was afraid to do it. Deborah was a judge in Israel at that time. She called him over and reminded him that God had promised to work a miracle if Barak would just obey. Barak agreed to go fight as God said, but he would only obey if Deborah went with him. Deborah agreed to go, but she told Barak he was silly to trust in a woman instead of God. She understood that no one is as wonderful and powerful as God.

Don't you think Deborah was a wise Princess? She knew that, even though it can sometimes be scary to do what God asks, it is always the best thing to do. The biggest blessings come when we believe what God says is true.

Prayer

Holy Spirit, help me to remember that God is the most wonderful and wise friend that I have!

Gideon's Army

T he Lord said to Gideon, "You have too many men to defeat the Midianites. I don't want the Israelites to brag that they saved themselves. So now, announce to the people, 'Anyone who is afraid may leave Mount Gilead. He may go back home.'" And 22,000 men went back home. But 10,000 remained.

Then the Lord said to Gideon, "There are still too many men. Take the men down to the water, and I will test them for you there."…

So Gideon led the men down to the water. There the Lord said to him,

"Separate them. Those who drink water by lapping it up like a dog will be in one group. Those who bend down to drink will be in the other group." There were 300 men who used their hands to bring water to their mouths. They lapped it as a dog does. All the rest got down on their knees to drink.

Then the Lord said to Gideon, "I will save you, using the 300 men who lapped the water. And I will allow you to defeat Midian. Let all the other men go to their homes." So Gideon sent the rest of Israel to their homes.

Sweet Dreams Devotion

Do you ever feel too small to serve God? Perhaps some of your friends are taller or seem smarter than you. Do you think God only uses the biggest, smartest people to work with him? Surprise! God loves to work through small people and tall people, girls with red hair and girls with brown hair, but especially those who are not very confident in their own abilities.

Just look at Gideon. God called him to fight against a very large army. Then he told Gideon to get rid of almost all of his soldiers. Only 300 of Gideon's men were invited to the fight.

Now that is scary!
But guess what? God defeated the enemies. Gideon's men simply obeyed orders to blow their trumpets and smash their jars. God confused their enemies and made them fight their own people. They tried to run, but were captured by Gideon's men.

Whenever you feel like something is too hard for you to do, thank God for it. Remember that he loves to be strong for you when you are weak.

Praise

God, you have chosen to use
all sorts of girls to serve you.
When I don't feel very strong,
thank you for being my strength!

Samson

JUDGES 16:4-6, 17-20

S amson fell in love with a woman named Delilah.... The kings of the Philistines went to Delilah. They said, "Try to find out what makes Samson so strong. Try to trick him into telling you. Find out how we could capture him and tie him up."...

So Delilah said to Samson, "Tell me why you are so strong. How could someone tie you up and take control of you?"...

He said, "I have never had my hair cut. I have been set apart to God as a Nazirite since I was born. If someone shaved my head, then I would lose my strength. I would become as weak as any other man."

Delilah saw that he had told her everything sincerely.... Delilah got Samson to go to sleep.... Then she called in a man to shave off the seven braids of Samson's hair. In this way she began to make him weak....

But he did not know that the Lord had left him.

Sweet Dreams Devotion

Do you know that, before you were born, God had big plans for you? Before Samson was even born, God had a special plan for his life. God wanted Samson to protect his people from the evil Philistines. So God gave Samson amazing strength. For a while Samson used his gift to destroy Israel's enemies. But after a while Samson became friends with the enemy. Because he stopped following the Lord, God caused Samson's strength to leave.

The good news is that Samson was very sorry and asked God to forgive him. He asked God to give him strength one last time to destroy many Philistines, as well as the temple and idol they worshiped in it. God forgave Samson and let him finish the work he was born to do.

What gift has God given you? Stay close to him and use the gifts he has given you to share his love with everyone you meet.

Prayer

Dear Jesus, help me to keep my eyes on you and always use my gifts to serve you. Help me to play a part in spreading your love to a needy world.

God Speaks to Samuel

1 SAMUEL 3:1-10

The boy Samuel served the Lord under Eli. In those days the Lord did not speak directly to people very often. There were very few visions....

One night [Eli] was lying in bed. Samuel was also in bed in the Lord's Holy Tent....

Then the Lord called Samuel. Samuel answered, "I am here!" He ran to Eli and said, "I am here. You called me."

But Eli said, "I didn't call you. Go back to bed." So Samuel went back to bed.

The Lord called again, "Samuel!"

Samuel again went to Eli and said, "I am here. You called me."

Again Eli said, "I didn't call you. Go back to bed."

Samuel did not yet know the Lord. The Lord had not spoken directly to him yet.

The Lord called Samuel for the third time. Samuel got up and went to Eli. He said, "I am here. You called me."

Then Eli realized the Lord was calling the boy. So he told Samuel, "Go to bed. If he calls you again, say, 'Speak, Lord. I am your servant, and I am listening.'" So Samuel went and lay down in bed.

The Lord came and stood there. He called as he had before....

Samuel said, "Speak, Lord. I am your servant, and I am listening."

listen

Sweet Dreams Devotion

Eli was a priest in the Temple of God and Samuel was his helper. Priests are supposed to hear messages from God, but there were very few words from God in those days. Samuel had never heard God's voice.

One night, when Samuel was sleeping, the Lord spoke to Samuel. Samuel thought it was Eli speaking. Three times this happened, when finally Eli realized God was talking to Samuel. He told Samuel to listen to the Lord and Samuel obeyed. He became Israel's prophet who would tell the people what the Lord wanted them to know.

Many Christians even today forget to listen to God. They are too busy to study the Bible or pray. They miss hearing his voice, like Eli did. We need to be like Samuel. Listen for God to speak to your heart. When he does, tell the Lord you are listening and willing to obey.

PROMISE:

God still speaks to his Princesses through the Bible and through our quiet times of **PRAYER** and praise!

The Boy David

1 SAMUEL 16:1, 4-5, 10-13

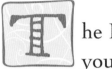he Lord said to Samuel…"Fill your container with olive oil and go. I am sending you to Jesse who lives in Bethlehem. I have chosen one of his sons to be king."…

Samuel did what the Lord told him to do.…

Then he made Jesse and his sons holy for the Lord. And he invited them to come to the sacrifice.…

Jesse had seven of his sons pass by Samuel. But Samuel said to him, "The Lord has not chosen any of these."

Then he asked Jesse, "Are these all the sons you have?"

Jesse answered, "I still have the youngest son. He is out taking care of the sheep."

Samuel said, "Send for him. We will not sit down to eat until he arrives."

So Jesse sent and had his youngest son brought in....

The Lord said to Samuel, "Go! Appoint him. He is the one."

So Samuel took the container of olive oil. Then he poured oil on Jesse's youngest son to appoint him in front of his brothers. From that day on, the Lord's Spirit entered David with power.

Sweet Dreams Devotion

David wasn't looking to be a big shot. He was just looking after his dad's sheep. He had no idea that God had big plans in store for a young shepherd boy. But God did.

God told Samuel to go to Jesse's house. God would show Samuel which one of Jesse's eight sons was God's choice for king. Jesse showed Samuel the oldest seven, who all looked very big and strong. But God didn't care what the man looked like on the outside. God wanted the person whose heart belonged to him. David was the one who followed after God's heart, and God chose David to be king.

People today care a lot about what they look like on the outside. That's alright, but God cares much more about our hearts. He wants to see that, deep inside, we love and obey God.

prayer

Dear Lord, please make me a person who follows after your heart too. I want to love and serve you more than anything else in the world.

David Fights Goliath

he Philistines had a champion fighter named Goliath. He was from Gath. He was about nine feet four inches tall....

Goliath stood and shouted to the Israelite soldiers... "Today I stand and dare the army of Israel! Send one of your men to fight me!" When Saul and the Israelites heard the Philistine's words, they were very afraid....

David said to Saul, "Don't let anyone be discouraged. I, your servant, will go and fight this Philistine!"...

He took his stick in his hand. And he chose five smooth stones from a stream. He put them in his pouch and held his sling in his hand. Then he went to meet Goliath....

Goliath looked at David. He saw that David was only a boy.... He said, "Do you think I am a dog, that you come at me with a stick?"...

But David said to him, "You come to me using a sword, a large spear and a small spear. But I come to you in the name of the Lord of heaven's armies. He's the God of the armies of Israel! You have spoken out against him. Today the Lord will give you to me.... Then all the world will know there is a God in Israel!"

Sweet Dreams Devotion

Goliath wasn't just big. He was really huge—like a great big, scary monster. He was bigger, braver, and stronger than anyone in Israel's army, and he loved to tease them about it.

Have you ever been bullied by someone bigger than you? It can be very scary. All of Israel's soldiers were very frightened.

David wasn't a part of the army. He was just a young shepherd boy. But he heard the mean things Goliath said to Israel and to God. David knew he was no match for Goliath on his own, but he also knew that God was on his side. He was sure to win.

Of course, David did win. God used one little rock from  David's sling to bring the giant Goliath down to his death. Like David, we can be sure that no matter how big any bully is, God is bigger, and he is always watching over us.

PRAISE:

I praise you, God, because you **PROTECT** me and fight for me. I can rest knowing that you take care of me!

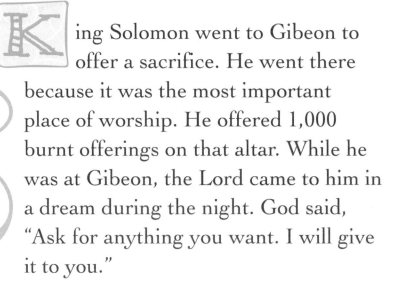

Solomon Asks for Wisdom

King Solomon went to Gibeon to offer a sacrifice. He went there because it was the most important place of worship. He offered 1,000 burnt offerings on that altar. While he was at Gibeon, the Lord came to him in a dream during the night. God said, "Ask for anything you want. I will give it to you."

Solomon answered, "You were very kind to your servant, my father David. He obeyed you. He was honest and lived right. And you showed great kindness to him when you allowed his son to be king after him. Lord my God, you have allowed me to be king in my father's place. But I am like a little child. I do not have the wisdom I need to do what I must do. I, your servant, am here among your chosen people. There are too many of them to count. So I ask that you give me wisdom. Then I can rule the people in the right way. Then I will know the differ- ence between right and wrong. Without wisdom, it is impossible to rule this great people of yours."

Sweet Dreams Devotion

If you could have any one thing in the world, what would you want? Would you want a puppy or a pony or your very own pink castle? God gave Solomon an amazing choice. He told Solomon to ask for whatever he wished.

Did he ask for money? Was he after fame or power? No, Solomon had been taught well by his parents. He knew that nothing in this world was worth as much as wisdom. He wanted to know how to rule God's people well, as king. So he asked for wisdom. God made Solomon the wisest man who ever lived. And God was so pleased with Solomon's choice, that he added fame and money to go with it.

God wants us to ask him for wisdom too. He is more than happy to teach us his truth, just like he did for Solomon.

Promise

God promises to give us wisdom to know right from wrong whenever we ask him for it.

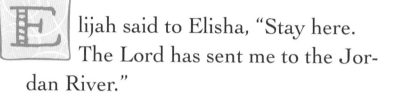

Elijah's Fiery Chariot

2 KINGS 2:6-12

Elijah said to Elisha, "Stay here. The Lord has sent me to the Jordan River."

Elisha answered, "As the Lord lives, and as you live, I won't leave you."

So the two of them went on. Fifty men from a group of the prophets came. They stood far from where Elijah and Elisha were by the Jordan. Elijah took off his coat. Then he rolled it up and hit the water. The water divided to the right and to the left. Then Elijah and Elisha crossed over on dry ground.

After they had crossed over, Elijah said to Elisha, "What can I do for you before I am taken from you?"

Elisha said, "Leave me a double share of your spirit."

Elijah said, "You have asked a hard thing. But if you see me when I am taken from you, it will be yours. If you don't, it won't happen."

Elijah and Elisha were still walking and talking. Then a chariot and horses of fire appeared. The chariot and horses of fire separated Elijah from Elisha. Then Elijah went up to heaven in a whirlwind. Elisha saw it and shouted, "My father! My father! The chariots of Israel and their horsemen!" Elisha did not see him anymore.

Sweet Dreams Devotion

Have you ever had to say good-bye to someone you loved as they left this earth for their wonderful home in heaven? Elisha did. He had worked so closely with the prophet Elijah that he called him his father.

One day, God said it was time for Elijah to go home to heaven. He told Elisha and the other prophets that it was going to happen. Even though Elisha knew that Elijah would be in a better place, he was still very sad. He was going to miss his friend. It's hard to say good-bye.

Lord, thank you for the promise of heaven. Thank you that you are **always** with us here on earth too.

Praise

God did take Elijah to heaven in a fiery chariot. But Elisha was not left alone. God answered his prayer and put his own spirit on Elisha. Elisha knew that God would always be with him, just like he had been with Elijah.

Josiah the Boy King

2 CHRONICLES 34:1-2, 29-33

Josiah was eight years old when he became king. He ruled 31 years in Jerusalem. He did what the Lord said was right. He did good things as his ancestor David had done. Josiah did not stop doing what was right....

The king gathered all the elders of Judah and Jerusalem together. He went up to the Temple of the Lord. All the men from Judah and the people from Jerusalem went with him. The priests and the Levites and all the people — from the most important to the least important — went with him. He read to them all the words in the Book of the

Agreement. That book was found in the Temple of the Lord. Then the king stood by his pillar. He made an agreement in the presence of the Lord. He agreed to follow the Lord and to obey his commands, rules and laws with his whole being. And he agreed to obey the words of the agreement written in this book. Then Josiah made all the people in Jerusalem and Benjamin promise to accept the agreement. The people of Jerusalem obeyed the agreement of God, the God their ancestors obeyed.

And Josiah...led everyone in Israel to serve the Lord their God. While Josiah lived, the people obeyed the Lord, the God their ancestors obeyed.

Sweet Dreams Devotion

Israel had been very bad. King after king had led the people to do the wrong thing by worshiping idols instead of the true God.

Then came Josiah. He was only eight years old when he became king. Imagine becoming a king when you are just in third grade! Josiah loved God with all his heart. He destroyed all the places where the people had set up idols. Then he paid workers to rebuild God's Temple that had fallen apart before Josiah became king.

When they were rebuilding the Temple, the people discovered secret treasure! They found the book of God's Word as it was told to Moses. Josiah heard for the first time what God had to say in his book. He had it read to all the people. The people of Israel were very sorry for the way they had treated God. God forgave his people.

PRAYER:

Lord, please teach me from your Word. Help me to know your ways and to **FOLLOW** them with my whole heart, just like Josiah.

Esther Becomes Queen

Mordecai had a cousin named Hadassah, who had no father or mother. So Mordecai took care of her. Hadassah was also called Esther, and she had a very pretty figure and face. Mordecai had adopted her as his own daughter when her father and mother died.

The king's command and order had been heard. And many girls had been brought to the palace in Susa....

Before a girl could take her turn with King Xerxes, she had to complete 12 months of beauty treatments. These were ordered for the women. For 6 months she was treated with oil and myrrh. And she spent 6 months with perfumes and cosmetics....

Esther daughter of Abihail, Mordecai's uncle, had been adopted by Mordecai. The time came for Esther to go to the king. She asked for only what Hegai suggested she should take. (Hegai was the king's eunuch who was in charge of the women.) And everyone who saw Esther liked her. So Esther was taken to King Xerxes in the royal palace....

And the king was pleased with Esther more than with any of the other virgins. And he liked her more than any of the others. So King Xerxes put a royal crown on Esther's head. And he made her queen.

Sweet Dreams Devotion

Did you know that God once saved Israel through the Miss Persia beauty pageant? Well, sort of. King Xerxes of Persia needed a new queen. His servants said he should have all the most beautiful girls in the kingdom to come before him. He could pick out whichever one he liked the best.

Xerxes didn't know it, but God had already picked the one. He had planned for Esther to become the next queen for an important reason. Esther was a Jew. She didn't tell anyone at first because some of the

Persians didn't like the Jews. But when Esther went before the king, he liked her more than the rest and made her the queen.

Later, a wicked man named Haman tried to have all the Jews in Persia killed. Esther learned about his evil plan and was able to save God's people because she was the queen.

prayer

Father, what good works do you have planned for me to do? Please show me so I can work with you to build your kingdom.

Great Prayer

PSALM 23:1-6

he Lord is my shepherd.
    I have everything I need.

He gives me rest in green pastures.
    He leads me to calm water.

He gives me new strength.
For the good of his name,
    he leads me on paths that are right.

Even if I walk
    through a very dark valley,
I will not be afraid
    because you are with me.

Your rod and your shepherd's staff
    comfort me.

You prepare a meal for me
  in front of my enemies.

You pour oil of blessing on my head.
  You give me more than I can hold.

Surely your goodness and love
    will be with me
  all my life.
And I will live in the house of the Lord
    forever.

Sweet Dreams Devotion

Do you know what David did before he was a king? Do you think he delivered pizza or dropped off newspapers from the back of a donkey? No, he was a shepherd! He spent many days out in the field taking care of his father's sheep. God taught David many good lessons when he was alone outside with the sheep. David began to understand that God was his shepherd too. He knew that God was good and gave David everything he needed to live well and enjoy God.

Psalm 23 is a great prayer that David wrote to help us remember that God takes care of us too. God says that we are like sheep, and Jesus is like our shepherd. He watches over us night and day. He leads us to the right places to learn about him. And he promises to take us home to heaven with him one day.

Praise

I praise you, Jesus, because you are my Great Shepherd. Thank you for protecting me and for staying close to me all the time.

A Time for Everything

ECCLESIASTES 3:1-8

There is a right time for everything.

Everything on earth has its special season.

There is a time to be born
and a time to die.

There is a time to plant
and a time to pull up plants.

There is a time to kill
and a time to heal.

There is a time to destroy
and a time to build.

There is a time to cry
and a time to laugh.

There is a time to be sad
   and a time to dance.

There is a time to throw away stones
   and a time to gather them.

There is a time to hug
   and a time not to hug.

There is a time to look for something
   and a time to stop looking for it.

There is a time to keep things
   and a time to throw things away.

There is a time to tear apart
   and a time to sew together.

There is a time to be silent
   and a time to speak.

There is a time to love
   and a time to hate.

Sweet Dreams Devotion

What do you like to do more than anything? Do you like to play with your friends? Ride your bike? Read funny stories? Sing out loud?

God has given us so many wonderful gifts in life. He loves us and is happy to see us enjoying the world he created. He has given you legs to jump, but not to jump inside your classroom. He has given you a mouth to speak, but not while your pastor is talking at church. He has given you family and friends to play with, but he has also asked you to help around the house.

God has given
us every good thing, and we need to
enjoy each one at the right time.

PRAISE:

Thank you, God, for
    making life so much **FUN**!
Help me to enjoy
    the best of all you have
for me at the right time.

Four Men in a Furnace

DANIEL 3:14-17, 21, 25-28

King Nebuchadnezzar said, "Shadrach, Meshach and Abednego...you must be ready to bow down and worship the statue I made.... But if you do not worship it, you will be thrown quickly into the blazing furnace...."

Shadrach, Meshach and Abednego... said, "Nebuchadnezzar, we do not need to defend ourselves to you. You can throw us into the blazing furnace. The God we serve is able to save us from the furnace and your power."...

So Shadrach, Meshach and Abednego were tied up and thrown into the blazing furnace....

The king said, "Look! I see four men. They are walking around in the fire. They are not tied up, and they are not burned. The fourth man looks like a son of the gods."

Then Nebuchadnezzar went to the opening of the blazing furnace. He shouted, "Shadrach, Meshach and Abednego, come out! Servants of the Most High God, come here!"

So Shadrach, Meshach and Abednego came out of the fire.... Their hair was not burned. Their robes were not burned. And they didn't even smell like smoke.

Then Nebuchadnezzar said, "Praise the God of Shadrach, Meshach and Abednego. Their God has sent his angel and saved his servants from the fire!"

Sweet Dreams Devotion

Have you ever roasted marshmallows over an open fire? Did you feel the heat on your skin as you sat beside it?

Shadrach, Meshach, and Abednego felt the heat of a fire once. Only, instead of marshmallows, they themselves were supposed to be roasted!

Shadrach, Meshach, and Abednego refused to bow down to the idol King Nebuchadnezzar made. They said they would only worship the true God. It made the king so very angry that he had them thrown inside a fiery furnace. It was so hot that it burned up the soldiers who threw them inside! But God's men weren't hurt. In fact, Nebuchadnezzar saw a fourth man walking around with the men inside! Jesus had come to protect them in the fiery place.

Nebuchadnezzar realized he had been worshiping the wrong god. He brought the men out of the fire and told his kingdom that they would now all serve the one, true God.

Prayer

Dear Jesus, help me to be brave like Shadrach, Meshach, and Abednego. I want to always stand up for you like they did, no matter what the cost.

Daniel in the Lions' Den

DANIEL 6:6-7, 9-10,
13, 16, 19-22

he supervisors and the governors went as a group to the king. They said:… "We think the king should make this law that everyone would have to obey: No one should pray to any god or man except to you, our king. This should be done for the next 30 days. Anyone who doesn't obey will be thrown into the lions' den…. So King Darius made the law and had it written.

When Daniel heard that the new law had been written, he went to his house…. He prayed and thanked God, just as he always had done.

Then those men spoke to the king. They said, "Daniel is…not paying attention to the law you wrote. Daniel still prays to his God three times every day."…

So King Darius gave the order. They brought Daniel and threw him into the lions' den. The king said to Daniel, "May the God you serve all the time save you!"…

The next morning King Darius…hurried to the lions' den. As he came near the den, he…called out to Daniel. He said, "Daniel, servant of the living God! Has your God that you always worship been able to save you from the lions?"

Daniel answered, "My king, live forever! My God sent his angel to close the lions' mouths. They have not hurt me."

faith

Sweet Dreams Devotion

Do you like to talk to God, Princess? Daniel loved to pray. He knelt down to talk to God three times every day. And God loved Daniel. But evil men in King Darius's kingdom hated Daniel and wanted him dead. They tricked King Darius into making a law that said everyone in the kingdom must only pray to the king. Daniel heard about the law, but kept on praying to God anyway.

The law said Daniel had to be thrown into a den of lions because he disobeyed. King Darius was very sad, but he couldn't help save Daniel. But guess

You are the God who **saves**! I praise you because you are good, and you have the **power** to do good for your people!

Praise

who could? That's right! God saved Daniel. He closed the hungry lions' mouths. The next day, King Darius rushed to the lions' den to see if Daniel had lived. Daniel told Darius that God had saved him. King Darius was so happy! He brought Daniel out and told everyone in the kingdom to only pray to Daniel's God from then on.

Jonah and the Big Fish

JONAH 1:3-5, 11-12, 15, 17

Jonah...went to the city of Joppa. There he found a ship that was going to the city of Tarshish.... He wanted to go to Tarshish to run away from the Lord.

But the Lord sent a great wind on the sea. This wind made the sea very rough. So the ship was in danger of breaking apart. The sailors were afraid....

The wind and the waves of the sea were becoming much stronger. So the men said to Jonah, "What should we do to you to make the sea calm down?"

Jonah said to them, "Pick me up, and throw me into the sea. Then it will calm down. I know it is my fault that this great storm has come on you."…

Then the men picked up Jonah and threw him into the sea. So the sea became calm.…

And the Lord caused a very big fish to swallow Jonah. Jonah was in the stomach of the fish three days and three nights.

calm

Sweet Dreams Devotion

Do you know what it means to repent? To repent means to admit that you are wrong. It means to ask God for forgiveness. When you are really sorry you stop doing the wrong thing and start doing what is right.

Nineveh was a city filled with people who ignored God. So God told Jonah to go to Nineveh. He wanted Jonah to warn the Ninevites that God would have to punish them if they didn't repent.

But there was a problem. Jonah didn't want to go to Nineveh. He didn't like those people, anyway. So he hopped on a boat going the other way. God stopped Jonah with a terrible storm. The people on the boat threw him overboard, where a giant fish swallowed him whole. Jonah realized that he needed to repent, just like the Ninevites. He turned back to God, and God saved him. Then God used Jonah to help save Nineveh too!

PRAISE:

Dear God, you are
so patient with me!
Thank you for your **GIFT**
of forgiveness.

Gabriel Visits Mary

God sent the angel Gabriel to a virgin who lived in Nazareth, a town in Galilee. She was engaged to marry a man named Joseph from the family of David. Her name was Mary. The angel came to her and said, "Greetings! The Lord has blessed you and is with you."

But Mary was very confused by what the angel said. Mary wondered, "What does this mean?"

The angel said to her, "Don't be afraid, Mary, because God is pleased with you. Listen! You will become pregnant. You will give birth to a son, and you will name him Jesus. He will be great, and people will call him the Son of the Most High. The Lord God will give him the throne of King David, his ancestor. He will rule over the people of Jacob forever. His kingdom will never end."

Mary said to the angel, "How will this happen? I am a virgin!"

The angel said to Mary, "The Holy Spirit will come upon you, and the power of the Most High will cover you. The baby will be holy. He will be called the Son of God...."

Mary said, "I am the servant girl of the Lord. Let this happen to me as you say!" Then the angel went away.

Sweet Dreams Devotion

Can you imagine how Mary must have felt? She was in her hometown of Nazareth. She was probably planning her wedding and working around the home as usual. All of a sudden, an angel appeared out of nowhere!

At first, she was frightened. Why had God sent an angel to her house? Gabriel, the angel, told her not to be scared because God had picked her to play a very special part of God's coming to earth. Back when Adam and Eve first sinned, God had promised to send someone who would save his people. After waiting thousands of years, the time had come. God had chosen Mary to be the mother of his only Son, Jesus. Jesus would save God's people from their sins.

She knew it wasn't going to be easy, but Mary agreed to God's plan. She belonged to God and was glad to serve him in this special way.

prayer

Lord, please make me willing to serve you in every way I can. I want to be a part of your kingdom work too!

Mary Visits Elizabeth

LUKE 1:35-37, 39-45

The angel said to Mary…"Now listen! Elizabeth, your relative, is very old. But she is also pregnant with a son. Everyone thought she could not have a baby, but she has been pregnant for six months. God can do everything!"…

Mary got up and went quickly to a town in the mountains of Judea. She went to Zechariah's house and greeted Elizabeth. When Elizabeth heard Mary's greeting, the unborn baby inside Elizabeth jumped. Then Elizabeth was filled with the Holy Spirit. She cried out in a loud voice, "God has

blessed you more than
any other woman. And
God has blessed the
baby which you will
give birth to. You
are the mother of my
Lord, and you have come
to me! Why has something
so good happened to me? When
I heard your voice, the baby inside
me jumped with joy. You are blessed
because you believed what the Lord
said to you would really happen."

joy

Sweet Dreams Devotion

Elizabeth was much older than Mary, and she was married to a man named Zechariah. Even though she was past the normal age to have a baby, God put a baby boy inside her. Her son was going to help prepare people's hearts so they would be ready for Jesus.

Both women were carrying these special babies in their tummies. One day Mary came to visit Elizabeth. As soon as Elizabeth saw Mary, the baby inside Elizabeth jumped for joy! Elizabeth realized right away that her baby was excited about Mary's baby inside her!

How could unborn babies know what was happening? God was at work. God caused the miracle to happen, and he let the two mommies experience it. It helped both women know that they were going to be a part of something really big and really special. They were both filled with thankfulness to God for his blessing.

PRAISE:

You are a God of miracles!
I praise you because your **PLAN** is better than any other one.
It makes me want to do a little **DANCE** too!

Baby Jesus Is Born

LUKE 2:1-7

At that time, Augustus Caesar sent an order to all people in the countries that were under Roman rule. The order said that they must list their names in a register. This was the first registration taken while Quirinius was governor of Syria. And everyone went to their own towns to be registered.

So Joseph left Nazareth, a town in Galilee. He went to the town of Bethlehem in Judea. This town was known as the town of David. Joseph went there because he was from the family of David. Joseph registered with Mary because she was engaged to marry him. (Mary was now pregnant.) While Joseph and Mary were in Bethlehem, the time came for her to have the baby. She gave birth to her first son. There were no rooms left in the inn. So she wrapped the baby with cloths and laid him in a box where animals are fed.

baby

Caesar Augustus wanted to know how many people he ruled over. It wasn't because he wanted to know how many birthday gifts he might need to buy; it was because he could make all those people pay taxes. So he told everybody to go back home where they came from and sign up. Joseph was from Bethlehem, so he and Mary loaded up a donkey and began the long journey.

What no one knew at the time was that God was at work. He was making his promise come true. Hundreds of years before Mary and Joseph, God's prophets said the Messiah would be

You are the God who keeps promises!
Thank you, **Jesus**, for coming to earth
as one of us to **save** us from our sins.

Praise

born in Bethlehem. They said he would
be born in a simple place, tucked up in
a manger.

Jesus' birth happened just like they
said. Mary and Joseph were not able
to find a room because the town was so
crowded. Instead, she gave birth to
Jesus in a stable alongside the animals.
What a humble way for God to bring
his own Son into the world!

Shepherds in Their Fields

LUKE 2:8-18

Some shepherds were in the fields nearby watching their sheep. An angel of the Lord stood before them. The glory of the Lord was shining around them, and suddenly they became very frightened. The angel said to them, "Don't be afraid, because I am bringing you some good news. It will be a joy to all the people. Today your Savior was born in David's town. He is Christ, the Lord. This is how you will know him: You will find a baby wrapped in cloths and lying in a feeding box."

Then a very large group of angels from

heaven joined the first angel. All the angels were praising God, saying:

"Give glory to God in heaven, and on earth let there be peace to the people who please God."

Then the angels left the shepherds and went back to heaven. The shepherds said to each other, "Let us go to Bethlehem and see this thing that has happened. We will see this thing the Lord told us about."

So the shepherds went quickly and found Mary and Joseph. And the shepherds saw the baby lying in a feeding box. Then they told what the angels had said about this child. Everyone was amazed when they heard what the shepherds said to them.

Sweet Dreams Devotion

The night was dark and cold. At first it seemed like any other night under the stars, watching the sheep. Then the angel appeared. God's glory began to shine all around the shepherds. They hardly knew what to think, but they did know that they were scared.

The angel told them not to be afraid. In fact, he wanted them to rejoice. A great day had come for God's people. The promised Savior from David's family had been born at last. Then the angel invited the shepherds to go see the little baby for themselves.

The angel was joined by thousands and thousands of other angels. They filled the night sky with beautiful praises to God for his goodness. Then the shepherds were amazed. They hurried to the place where Jesus was, and they worshiped him.

Prayer

Lord Jesus, you invite everyone to come to you. I come before you now, just like the shepherds, and worship you.

The Wise Men Visit Jesus

MATTHEW 2:1-2, 8-12

Jesus was born in the town of Bethlehem in Judea during the time when Herod was king. After Jesus was born, some wise men from the east came to Jerusalem. They asked, "Where is the baby who was born to be the king of the Jews? We saw his star in the east. We came to worship him."...

Herod sent the wise men to Bethlehem. He said to them, "Go and look carefully to find the child. When you find him, come tell me. Then I can go worship him too."

The wise men heard the king and then left. They saw the same star they had

seen in the east. It went before them until it stopped above the place where the child was. When the wise men saw the star, they were filled with joy. They went to the house where the child was and saw him with his mother, Mary. They bowed down and worshiped the child. They opened the gifts they brought for him. They gave him treasures of gold, frankincense, and myrrh. But God warned the wise men in a dream not to go back to Herod. So they went home to their own country by a different way.

Sweet Dreams Devotion

Have you ever been out in the country late at night? Did you look up at the stars in the sky? The further away from city lights you are, the brighter they seem to shine.

A long time ago, some very wise men had been looking up at the stars. They had been waiting and searching for one special star. They knew when that star appeared in the sky, the Savior of the world had come. At last, they saw it! They loaded their camels and traveled west, following the star all the way to Bethlehem. When they found Jesus, he was still a little boy. Yet the wise men gave him very costly gifts fit for a king. Even though Jesus was just a boy, the wise men knew he was the King who came to save them. The grown men knelt down and worshiped Jesus.

PRAYER:

Dear Jesus, thank you for the beautiful stars you made. Every time I see a **STAR**, help me to remember to worship you.

Where Did He Go?

LUKE 2:41-50

Every year Jesus' parents went to Jerusalem for the Passover Feast. When Jesus was 12 years old, they went to the feast as they always did. When the feast days were over, they went home. The boy Jesus stayed behind in Jerusalem, but his parents did not know it. Joseph and Mary traveled for a whole day. They thought that Jesus was with them in the group. Then they began to look for him among their family and friends, but they did not find him. So they went back to Jerusalem to look for him there. After three days they found him. Jesus was sitting in the Temple with the religious teachers, listening to them and asking them questions. All who heard him were amazed at his understanding and wise answers. When Jesus' parents saw him, they were amazed. His mother said to him, "Son, why did you do this to us? Your father and I were very worried about you. We have been looking for you."

Jesus asked, "Why did you have to look for me? You should have known that I must be where my Father's work is!" But they did not understand the meaning of what he said.

teach

Sweet Dreams Devotion

Have you ever been separated from your mom or dad just for a moment? That happened to Jesus when he was twelve years old, and his mom and dad were in a panic. They couldn't find him! He was supposed to be traveling home with them from their trip to Jerusalem, but he was nowhere to be found. They searched for three long days. At last they found him in the Temple courts asking the teachers questions. Mary and Joseph couldn't believe it. "We were so worried!" they said.

Jesus reminded them that he was not just an ordinary son. He was God's Son. He belonged in his Father's house. It was hard for Mary and Joseph to remember that the same boy they were raising was also the promised Messiah. But Mary took the lesson to heart and learned to trust God more.

Are you looking for Jesus, too? You will find him when you seek him in prayer and in his Word.

promise

God promises that we will find him when we seek him with all our hearts.

John Baptizes Jesus

MATTHEW 3:1-2, 4-6, 13-17

bout that time John the Baptist came and began preaching in the desert area of Judea. John said, "Change your hearts and lives because the kingdom of heaven is coming soon."...

John's clothes were made from camel's hair. He wore a leather belt around his waist. For food, he ate locusts and wild honey. Many people went to hear John preach. They came from Jerusalem and all Judea and all the area around the Jordan River. They told of the sins they had done, and John baptized them in the Jordan River....

At that time Jesus came from Galilee to the Jordan River. He came to John and wanted John to baptize him. But John tried to stop him. John said, "Why do you come to me to be baptized? I should be baptized by you!"

Jesus answered, "Let it be this way for now. We should do all things that are right." So John agreed to baptize Jesus.

Jesus was baptized and came up out of the water. Heaven opened, and he saw God's Spirit coming down on him like a dove. And a voice spoke from heaven. The voice said, "This is my Son and I love him. I am very pleased with him."

Sweet Dreams Devotion

How would you like some slow-roasted grasshoppers for breakfast? No? John the Baptist would have liked it. He ate locusts and honey all the time.

Of course, John was very different from most people. He wore clothes made of camel skin. He always told the people to repent and turn back to God. Then he baptized them. And surprisingly, people came from all over to hear this strange man.

One day Jesus came to the river too. He told John to baptize him. John didn't want to do it. John wanted Jesus to baptize him instead. But Jesus said it had to be done that way. John baptized Jesus, and God opened the heavens. The Holy Spirit flew down to Jesus in the form of a dove and landed on Jesus' shoulder. God spoke out loud and said that he was pleased with Jesus, his Son. John and the others realized that Jesus was their long-awaited Savior.

PRAISE:

Jesus, I praise you because
you are perfect in every way.
You have pleased the Father
and you make me
PERFECT in his sight too.

Jesus is Tempted

The devil came to Jesus to tempt him. The devil said, "If you are the Son of God, tell these rocks to become bread."

Jesus answered, "It is written in the Scriptures, 'A person does not live only by eating bread. But a person lives by everything the Lord says.'"

Then the devil led Jesus to the holy city of Jerusalem. He put Jesus on a very high place of the Temple. The devil said, "If you are the Son of God, jump off....

Jesus answered him, "It also says in the Scriptures, 'Do not test the Lord your God.'"

Then the devil led Jesus to the top of a very high mountain. He showed Jesus all the kingdoms of the world and all the great things that are in those kingdoms. The devil said, "If you will bow down and worship me, I will give you all these things."

Jesus said to the devil, "Go away from me, Satan! It is written in the Scriptures, 'You must worship the Lord your God. Serve only him!'"

So the devil left Jesus. And then some angels came to Jesus and helped him.

Sweet Dreams Devotion

Imagine going all day without any food. Then your mom puts a plate of cookies in front of you, but tells you not to eat any. Would you be tempted to eat one anyway? Me too!

Jesus faced even greater temptations than we do. Once he went out to the desert. For 40 days, he didn't eat any food. Satan saw that he was weak and hungry and came to Jesus. He hoped he could trick him into sinning. He tried three times to get Jesus to follow him instead of his Father. Each time Satan tried,

Jesus told Satan God's truth by quoting a verse from the Bible. At last, Satan gave up. Jesus left the desert as pure and perfect as he had always been.

When you are tempted to sin, don't give in to Satan. Instead, pray to Jesus. He understands and will help you make the right choice.

Prayer

Dear Holy Spirit, please help me to remember God's Word so I can fight Satan when he tries to trick me too.

Story of the Sower

Jesus went out of the house and sat by the lake. Large crowds gathered around him. So Jesus got into a boat and sat, while the people stayed on the shore. Then Jesus used stories to teach them many things. He said: "A farmer went out to plant his seed. While he was planting, some seed fell by the road. The birds came and ate all that seed. Some seed fell on rocky ground, where there wasn't enough dirt. That seed grew very fast, because the ground was not deep. But when the sun rose, the plants dried up because they did not have deep roots. Some other seed fell among thorny weeds. The weeds grew and choked the good plants. Some other seed fell on good ground where it grew and became grain. Some plants made 100 times more grain. Other plants made 60 times more grain, and some made 30 times more grain. Let those with ears use them and listen!"

Sweet Dreams Devotion

If you wanted to plant a garden, would you do it on your driveway? No! You'd look for a nice, sunny spot with soft earth to plant your seeds.

Jesus says that his Word is like a seed. It needs a soft place to grow too. But people's hearts aren't always soft, or teachable. Some people hear God's truth, but Satan keeps them from understanding it. Some people hear and understand, but they don't obey what they know. Others hear about Jesus and believe him at first, but then they let what they want become more important than doing the right thing.

God wants us to have hearts like a soft garden. We take in God's Word, listen to him, and obey. We learn more and more about God and tell him that we are sorry for our sins to keep our lives free from "sin-weeds." Then we will blossom with God's love for him and others.

PRAYER:

Dear Jesus, please give me
a teachable **HEART**.
Help me to see any weeds
that need pulling in my life.
I want to **GROW** strong in you.

Jesus Walks on Water

MATTHEW 14:22-27

J esus made his followers get into the boat. He told them to go ahead of him to the other side of the lake. Jesus stayed there to tell the people they could go home. After he said good-bye to them, he went alone up into the hills to pray. It was late, and Jesus was there alone. By this time, the boat was already far away on the lake. The boat was having trouble because of the waves, and the wind was blowing against it.

Between three and six o'clock in the morning, Jesus' followers were still in the boat. Jesus came to them. He was

walking on the water. When the followers saw him walking on the water, they
were afraid. They said, "It's a ghost!"
and cried out in fear.

But Jesus quickly spoke to them.
He said, "Have courage!
It is I! Don't
be afraid."

Sweet Dreams Devotion

Once Jesus wanted time to be alone and pray. So he sent his followers away in a boat. They thought they would just sail across without any problems, but Jesus had a lesson for them to learn. The wind grew strong and the waves fought against the boat, and they were scared. They were in the middle of the sea when they suddenly saw Jesus walking toward them on the water! Peter wanted to be with Jesus so much that he got out of the boat to go to him. At first Peter walked on the water like Jesus. But when he stopped looking at Jesus and started worrying

Dear Jesus, help me not to get **worried** when bad things happen. Remind me to **trust** you to take care of me.

about the waves, he began to sink. Jesus had to save him.

We sometimes worry about a lot of things, just like Peter did. Jesus wants us to keep our eyes on him. When you're afraid, take time out to pray. Will you keep your eyes on the problem or on Jesus?

Jesus Blesses the Children

MARK 10:13-16

S ome people brought their small children to Jesus so he could touch them. But his followers told the people to stop bringing their children to him. When Jesus saw this, he was displeased. He said to them, "Let the little children come to me. Don't stop them. The kingdom of God belongs to people who are like these

little children. I tell you
the truth. You must
accept the kingdom of
God as a little child
accepts things, or
you will never

enter it." Then Jesus took the
children in his arms. He put
his hands on them and
blessed them.

accept

Sweet Dreams Devotion

Crowds of people followed Jesus everywhere he went. People wanted to touch him, see him, and talk to him all the time. But when some parents began bringing their children to Jesus, his followers got mad. Jesus didn't have time for little kids, they thought. He needed to spend all his time with the grown-ups!

Boy, were they wrong! Jesus told his followers that he wanted the children to come to him. He loved them and put his hands on them and blessed them. Then he told the crowd that everybody needed to come to him just as a child would. He wanted them to believe him and have a simple loving faith like a child.

Isn't it great to know that Jesus loves you and blesses you, just like he did the children back then? Tell Jesus you want to be as close to him as you can.

promise

God says that
the kingdom of God belongs
to his children!

Jesus Clears the Temple

J esus went into the Temple. He threw out all the people who were buying and selling there. He turned over the tables that belonged to the men who were exchanging different kinds of money. And he upset the benches of those who were selling doves. Jesus said to all the people there, "It is written in the Scriptures, 'My Temple will be a house where people will pray.' But you are changing God's house into a 'hide-out for robbers.'"

The blind and crippled people came to Jesus in the Temple, and Jesus healed them. The leading priests and the teachers of the law saw that Jesus was doing wonderful things. They saw the children praising him in the Temple. The children were saying, "Praise to the Son of David." All these things made the priests and the teachers of the law very angry.

They asked Jesus, "Do you hear the things these children are saying?"

Jesus answered, "Yes. Haven't you read in the Scriptures, 'You have taught children and babies to sing praises'?"

Then Jesus left and went out of the city to Bethany, where he spent the night.

Sweet Dreams Devotion

When you think of Jesus in your mind, what do you see? Is he gentle, kind, and smiling?

Jesus was very kind and helpful. He also loved his heavenly Father more than anything. When he saw how the religious leaders and people had ruined his Father's Temple, his smile went away. He became very angry. He took a whip and made all the sellers who were cheating the people leave the Temple.

Do you ever get mad? We usually get angry when we don't get our way. But

Jesus isn't like us. When Jesus got angry, it was always for the right reason. He was protecting God's house and the people coming to worship him there.

PRAISE:

I praise you, Jesus, because you showed perfect **LOVE** for your Father. Help me to do the same!

Jesus Chooses His Apostles

T hen Jesus went up on a hill and called some men to come to him. These were the men Jesus wanted, and they went up to him. Jesus chose 12 men and called them apostles. He wanted these 12 to be with him, and he wanted to send them to other places to preach. He also wanted them to have the power to force demons out of people. These are the 12 men he chose: Simon (Jesus gave him the name Peter); James and John, the sons of Zebedee (Jesus gave them the name Boanerges, which means "Sons of Thunder"); Andrew,

Philip, Bartholomew, Matthew, Thomas, James the son of Alphaeus, Thaddaeus, Simon the Zealot, and Judas Iscariot. Judas is the one who gave Jesus to his enemies.

Sweet Dreams Devotion

Have you ever played a game where you had to pick a team? What would you look for? Perhaps you would choose the girls that you knew you could trust or count on. Jesus did the very same thing one day. He went to the mountain on a very special mission to choose twelve men to be his best friends and followers. He told them they would be his apostles who would work for God and preach the good news of Jesus to everyone. He would build his heavenly kingdom through their work on earth.

Jesus calls you to follow him too. Will you come to him, just like his apostles did? Jesus has a job for you to do. He wants you to share the good news of Jesus with those around you. Take a moment to think of anyone you know who doesn't know Jesus. Pray for them now, and ask God to give you a chance to tell that person the good news.

Praise

I thank you, Jesus, because you chose me to belong to you! I want to share your love with everyone I meet.

Jesus Calms the Storm

 hat evening, Jesus said to his followers, "Come with me across the lake." He and the followers left the people there. They went in the boat that Jesus was already sitting in. There were also other boats with them. A very strong wind came up on the lake. The waves began coming over the sides and into the boat. It was almost full of water. Jesus was at the back of the boat, sleeping with his head on a pillow. The followers went to him and woke him. They said, "Teacher, do you care about us? We will drown!"

Jesus stood up and commanded the wind and the waves to stop. He said, "Quiet! Be still!" Then the wind stopped, and the lake became calm.

Jesus said to his followers, "Why are you afraid? Do you still have no faith?"

The followers were very afraid and asked each other, "What kind of man is this? Even the wind and the waves obey him!"

obey

Sweet Dreams Devotion

Jesus' followers were in a boat on the Sea of Galilee. Suddenly a huge storm came up and shook the boat. The waves splashed over the edges of the boat, and the followers were very scared. Where was Jesus? He was taking a nap! They woke Jesus up and asked him, "How can you go on sleeping when we are all about to die? Don't you care about us?"

Do you think Jesus cared about his followers? Of course he did! He was teaching them another lesson. He spoke to the wind and the waves and told them to be still. His creation

I praise you, Jesus, because all of **creation** obeys you. You are Lord over all the earth!

Praise

obeyed him, and his followers were amazed. Jesus wanted them to know that they don't ever have to be afraid. And neither do we. We have the God of creation as our Savior and friend. We just need to keep our eyes on him and know that he is in control of all things.

The Blind Man Sees

MARK 10:46-52

Then they came to the town of Jericho. As Jesus was leaving there with his followers and a large crowd, a blind beggar named Bartimaeus (son of Timaeus) was sitting by the road. He heard that Jesus from Nazareth was walking by. The blind man cried out, "Jesus, Son of David, please help me!"

Many people scolded the blind man and told him to be quiet. But he shouted more and more, "Son of David, please help me!"

Jesus stopped and said, "Tell the man to come here."

So they called the blind man. They said, "Cheer up! Get to your feet. Jesus is calling you." The blind man stood up quickly. He left his coat there and went to Jesus.

Jesus asked him, "What do you want me to do for you?"

The blind man answered, "Teacher, I want to see again."

Jesus said, "Go. You are healed because you believed." At once the man was able to see again, and he followed Jesus on the road.

believe

Sweet Dreams Devotion

Have you ever met a blind person? Perhaps you have seen someone who is blind being led along by a seeing-eye dog as their helper. Bartimaeus didn't have a dog to help him. Every day he begged for money by the side of the road. In those days, it was the only way a blind person could make money to live.

One day Jesus came by his well-worn spot. Bartimaeus couldn't see Jesus, but he had heard all about him. He didn't want to let the moment slip by. He yelled out at the top of his lungs for Jesus to help him. People around him told him to be quiet, but he just yelled louder. Jesus called for the blind man. As he stood before Jesus, Jesus asked him what he wanted. Bartimaeus simply said he wanted to see. So Jesus healed him.

Do you have any needs like Bartimaeus? Don't be quiet about it. Talk to God out loud like you would if you were Bartimaeus by the side of the road. Call out to God and he will answer you.

PRAYER:

Dear God, thank you
for noticing me.
You hear me when I call,
and you always **HELP** me.

Poor Widow Gives All

J esus sat near the Temple money box where people put their gifts. He watched the people put in their money. Many rich people gave large sums of money. Then a poor widow came and gave two very small copper coins. These coins were not worth even a penny.

Jesus called his followers to him. He said, "I tell you the truth. This poor widow gave only two small coins. But she really gave more than all those rich people. The rich have plenty; they gave only what they did not need. This woman is very poor. But she gave all she had. And she needed that money to help her live."

Sweet Dreams Devotion

Jesus was watching the people as they came to the Temple. He noticed how the rich people threw in large amounts of money into the Temple's offering plate. Then a poor widow came and put in two coins. He brought his apostles close to notice the different gifts. Which was worth more, the rich people's gifts or the widow's two coins?

The rich people felt like their gift was better because it was more. Jesus said that it wasn't. The rich people had a lot more money they could have given, but they didn't. The widow, though, gave everything she had. God is pleased when we trust him enough to give with our whole hearts. He doesn't care about the amount.

Do you feel like you don't have anything to give to God? You do! Even if you don't have any money, you can give him time praying, serving, and learning his Word.

prayer

Dear Jesus, help me to have a giving heart. Show me how I can give my best to you, like the widow.

The Big Catch

LUKE 5:2-10

Jesus saw two boats at the shore of the lake. The fishermen had left them and were washing their nets. Jesus got into one of the boats, the one which belonged to Simon. Jesus asked Simon to push off a little from the land. Then Jesus sat down in the boat and... said to Simon, "Take the boat into deep water. If you will put your nets in the water, you will catch some fish."

Simon answered, "Master, we worked hard all night trying to catch fish, but we caught nothing. But you say to put the nets in the water; so I will." The fishermen did as Jesus told them. And they caught so many fish that the nets began to break. They called to their friends in the other boat to come and help them. The friends came, and both boats were filled so full that they were almost sinking.

 The fishermen were all amazed at the many fish they caught. When Simon Peter saw what had happened, he bowed down before Jesus and said, "Go away from me, Lord. I am a sinful man!"...

Jesus said to Simon, "Don't be afraid. From now on you will be fishermen for men."

Sweet Dreams Devotion

Jesus was in a boat with Peter, James, and John. The men had fished all night, but didn't catch anything.

Then Jesus told the men to put out their nets again. Even though they were very tired, they did what Jesus said anyway. This time the nets were filled with so many fish they had to get help pulling the nets to shore! Peter told Jesus he was too sinful to be near someone as good as Jesus. But Jesus invited him to be an apostle, one of his closest friends. He told the men they would now catch people instead of fish. He meant that they would teach people the truth about God's plan for saving them from their sins.

Even though we are sinners, Jesus wants us to tell others about him too. Jesus will use us to bring other people to him!

Promise

Our job is just to tell others about Jesus. God is the only one who can change their hearts.

Jesus Heals People

LUKE 8:41-45, 47-48,
51-52, 54-56

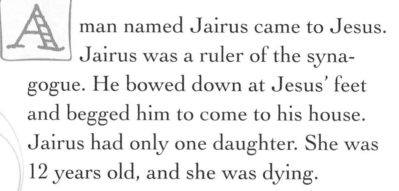

A man named Jairus came to Jesus. Jairus was a ruler of the synagogue. He bowed down at Jesus' feet and begged him to come to his house. Jairus had only one daughter. She was 12 years old, and she was dying.

While Jesus was on his way to Jairus' house, the people were crowding all around him. A woman was there who had been bleeding for 12 years. She had spent all her money on doctors, but no doctor was able to heal her. The woman came up behind Jesus and touched the edge of his coat. At that moment, her bleeding stopped. Then Jesus said, "Who touched me?"...

When the woman saw that she could not hide, she came forward, shaking. She bowed down before Jesus. While all the people listened, she told why she had touched him. Then, she said, she was healed immediately. Jesus said to her, "Dear woman, you are healed because you believed. Go in peace."...

Jesus went to the house.... All the people were crying and feeling sad because the girl was dead....

But Jesus took her by the hand and called to her, "My child, stand up!" Her spirit came back into her, and she stood up immediately. Jesus said, "Give her something to eat." The girl's parents were amazed.

Sweet Dreams Devotion

Have you ever seen the way some people follow famous people trying to get their autographs? Well Jesus had a crowd of people following him everywhere he went. They got so close, they almost crushed him! So how did Jesus know that someone very special had touched him? Jesus is God! He knew exactly what had happened to the sick woman. He just wanted her to stop hiding and know that God saw her need and wanted to heal her.

Then Jesus performed another amazing miracle. Jairus' daughter had died.

Everyone was crying. But Jesus took the girl by the hand and raised her back to life. Nothing was too difficult for him!

Do you ever feel like God is too important to notice you? So many people live on the earth. How can he keep track of them all? God says he knows how many hairs are on your head. He sees you and loves you more than you will ever know.

PROMISE:

God says that he loves you so much he has written your **NAME** on the palm of his hand!

The Lost Sheep and Coin

Many tax collectors and "sinners" came to listen to Jesus. The Pharisees and the teachers of the law began to complain: "Look! This man welcomes sinners and even eats with them!"

Then Jesus told them this story: "Suppose one of you has 100 sheep, but he loses 1 of them. Then he will leave the other 99 sheep alone and go out and look for the lost sheep. The man will keep on searching for the lost sheep until he finds it. And when he finds it, the man is very happy. He puts it on his shoulders and goes home. He calls to his friends and neighbors and says, 'Be happy with me because I found my lost sheep!' In the same way, I tell you there is much joy in heaven when 1 sinner changes his heart. There is more joy for that 1 sinner than there is for 99 good people who don't need to change.

"Suppose a woman has ten silver coins, but she loses one of them. She will light a lamp and clean the house. She will look carefully for the coin until she finds it. And when she finds it, she will call her friends and neighbors and say, 'Be happy with me because I have found the coin that I lost!' In the same way, there is joy before the angels of God when 1 sinner changes his heart."

Sweet Dreams Devotion

What would you do if you lost your favorite toy? Wouldn't you search and search until you found it?

God feels the same way about us. Jesus told a story about a shepherd who had 100 sheep. One day, the shepherd saw that one sheep was missing! He searched hard until he found it. When he did, he told everyone how happy he was.

Then Jesus told a similar story about a woman who lost a gold coin. She searched her whole house. When she found it, she threw a party!

When we do the wrong thing, we are like the sheep that wanders off or the coin that gets lost. Isn't it incredible that God comes looking for us, like the shepherd and the woman in the story? When we turn from our sin, our friendship with God is connected again. God rejoices when we are truly sorry!

Promise

God promises to be faithful to us, even when we wander away from the right path. He cares so much for each of his Princesses that he looks for us when we are lost.

The Son Who Left Home

esus said, "A man had two sons. The younger son said to his father, 'Give me my share of the property.' So the father divided the property between his two sons. Then the younger son gathered up all that was his and left. He traveled far away to another country. There he wasted his money in foolish living.... The son was hungry and needed money. So he got a job with one of the citizens there. The man sent the son into the fields to feed pigs. The son was so hungry that he was willing to eat the food the pigs were eating. But no one gave him anything. The son realized that he had been very foolish.... So the son left and went to his father.

Welcome Home

"While the son was still a long way off, his father saw him coming. He felt sorry for his son. So the father ran to him, and hugged and kissed him. The son said, 'Father, I have sinned against God and against you. I am not good enough to be called your son.' But the father said to his servants…'My son was dead, but now he is alive again! He was lost, but now he is found!' So they began to celebrate."

Sweet Dreams Devotion

Do you ever find it hard to understand just how much God loves you? Jesus knew the people around him would have a hard time understanding God's love. So he explained God's heart through a story about a rebellious son. In the story, there is a good and loving father with two sons. One stays home, but the other demands money and goes away to spend it foolishly. After he spent all the money, he realized he made a mistake. He decided to go home and see if his dad would let him come back as a servant instead of a son. But his dad surprised everybody. He ran

You are the God who forgives! Thank you, Father, for always **welcoming** me back into your arms.

Praise

to greet him on the road because he had been watching for him. Then he threw the boy a party! He was so glad to have his son home again.

Whenever we go against God, we need to remember Jesus' story. God welcomes us back to himself with open arms if we will simply run back to him and tell him how sorry we are.

Jesus Heals the Lepers

LUKE 17:11-19

Jesus was on his way to Jerusalem. Traveling from Galilee to Samaria, he came into a small town. Ten men met him there. These men did not come close to Jesus, because they all had a harmful skin disease. But they called to him, "Jesus! Master! Please help us!"

When Jesus saw the men, he said, "Go and show yourselves to the priests."

While the ten men were going, they were healed. When one of them saw that he was healed, he went back to Jesus. He praised God in a loud voice. Then he bowed down at Jesus' feet and thanked him. (This man was a Samaritan.) Jesus asked, "Ten men were healed; where are the other nine? Is this Samaritan the only one who came back to thank God?" Then Jesus said to him, "Stand up and go on your way. You were healed because you believed."

thanks

Sweet Dreams Devotion

Have you ever had to stay home from school or church because you had a fever, and your mom didn't want other people to get sick? Jesus told this story about people like that. The men stood off at a distance because they were not allowed to be near the healthy people. The men had a skin disease that others didn't want to catch. It was awful for them. So when they saw Jesus passing by, they cried out for help. Jesus heard them and told them to go see the priest or pastor. When they obeyed, their skin cleared up. They were healed.

Even though ten men had been healed, only one came back to thank Jesus for the miracle. Jesus was disappointed that the other men forgot to thank God.

Every good thing in our lives comes from the Lord. We need to remember his goodness and thank God for all the ways he shows us his love.

PRAYER:

Lord, please forgive me
when I have an unthankful heart.
I want you to know
that I am **THANKFUL**
for you and your goodness to me!

Jesus and Zacchaeus

LUKE 19:1-10

Jesus was going through the city of Jericho. In Jericho there was a man named Zacchaeus. He was a wealthy, very important tax collector. He wanted to see who Jesus was, but he was too short to see above the crowd. He ran ahead to a place where he knew Jesus would come. He climbed a sycamore tree so he could see Jesus. When Jesus came to that place, he looked up and saw Zacchaeus in the tree. He said to him, "Zacchaeus, hurry and come down! I must stay at your house today."

Zacchaeus came down quickly. He was pleased to have Jesus in his house. All the people saw this and began to complain, "Look at the kind of man Jesus stays with. Zacchaeus is a sinner!"

 But Zacchaeus said to the Lord, "I will give half of my money to the poor. If I have cheated anyone, I will pay that person back four times more!"

Jesus said, "Salvation has come to this house today. This man truly belongs to the family of Abraham. The Son of Man came to find lost people and save them."

Sweet Dreams Devotion

What does it mean to be truly sorry for what you did? Just look at the story of Zacchaeus.

Zacchaeus was a wealthy tax collector. But he had made a lot of his money by cheating people and making them pay more taxes than they should.

One day Jesus came into his town. Zacchaeus was so short he had to climb a tree to see above the crowds. Then Jesus looked up at Zacchaeus in the tree. Jesus told him to come down because he was going to Zacchaeus's house. Zacchaeus welcomed Jesus into his home. Then he told Jesus that he was very sorry for the wrong things he had done. He told Jesus he would give away half of all his money. If he had cheated anyone out of money, he would pay that person back four times as much as he took. Zacchaeus showed by his actions that he was truly sorry for his sin. And Jesus forgave him!

prayer

Lord, please help me to be truly sorry for my sins. I want to please you in everything I do.

Jesus and Nicodemus

There was a man named Nicodemus who was one of the Pharisees. He was an important Jewish leader. One night Nicodemus came to Jesus. He said, "Teacher, we know that you are a teacher sent from God. No one can do the miracles you do, unless God is with him."

Jesus answered, "I tell you the truth. Unless you are born again, you cannot be in God's kingdom."

Nicodemus said, "But if a man is already old, how can he be born again? He cannot enter his mother's body again. So how can he be born a second time?"

But Jesus answered, "I tell you the truth. Unless you are born from water and the Spirit, you cannot enter God's kingdom. A person's body is born from his human parents. But a person's spiritual life is born from the Spirit. Don't be surprised when I tell you, 'You must all be born again.' The wind blows where it wants to go. You hear the wind blow. But you don't know where the wind comes from or where it is going. It is the same with every person who is born from the Spirit."

Sweet Dreams Devotion

Nicodemus was a Pharisee. That means he was a member of the largest religious and political group at that time. Most Pharisees didn't like Jesus, but Nicodemus believed Jesus was sent from God. He visited Jesus at night, when no one else was around him so he could ask Jesus some questions. He told the Lord that he knew Jesus must be from God because of his miracles.

Jesus answered Nicodemus in a strange way. He told him that a man had to be born again to be saved! Nicodemus didn't understand. Certainly he couldn't get inside his mother's tummy again! So Jesus explained. We are born again when we realize how much we need Jesus. We stop trying to cover our sins and ask Jesus for forgiveness instead. Jesus alone can give us new life here on earth and forever in heaven.

PROMISE:

Jesus said that everyone
is born one time as a baby.
Those who **TRUST** Jesus
as their Savior
have a second birthday.

Do you have one birthday or **TWO?**

Jesus Feeds 5,000

JOHN 6:3-5, 7-13

 esus went up on a hill and there sat down with his followers. It was almost the time for the Jewish Passover Feast.

Jesus looked up and saw a large crowd coming toward him. He said to Philip, "Where can we buy bread for all these people to eat?"...

Philip answered, "Someone would have to work almost a year to buy enough bread for each person here to have only a little piece."...

Andrew said, "Here is a boy with five loaves of barley bread and two little fish.

But that is not enough for so many people."

Jesus said, "Tell the people to sit down." This was a very grassy place. There were about 5,000 men who sat down there. Then Jesus took the loaves of bread. He thanked God for the bread and gave it to the people who were sitting there. He did the same with the fish. He gave them as much as they wanted.

They all had enough to eat. When they had finished, Jesus said to his followers, "Gather the pieces of fish and bread that were not eaten. Don't waste anything." So they gathered up the pieces that were left. They filled 12 large baskets with the pieces that were left of the five barley loaves.

Sweet Dreams Devotion

Can you imagine 5,000 people coming to your house for supper? I think your mom might faint! The apostles looked out at the crowd in front of them. More than 5,000 hungry faces stared back at them. How were they ever going to be able to obey Jesus this time? He wanted the apostles to feed all those people, but they knew they didn't have enough money or food to do it.

Then Andrew told Jesus he had found one little boy willing to share his lunch. It was five barley loaves and two fish. But what good is a handful of food for so many people?

Jesus changed the young boy's gift into a gigantic miracle. After Jesus prayed, they passed the food around. Every person ate until they were full. They even had twelve baskets of food left over. The boy and the apostles learned an important lesson. All we are asked to do is bring what we have to Jesus, and he will do the rest. We do what we can to serve him, and he does what only he can do.

Prayer

Dear Jesus, I ask that you would work mighty miracles through me too. Help me to be willing to give whatever I can to help your kingdom grow.

Lazarus

JOHN 11:1, 3-5, 17,
21-23, 38-39, 41, 43-44

There was a man named Lazarus who was sick.... So Mary and Martha sent someone to tell Jesus, "Lord, the one you love is sick."

When Jesus heard this he said, "This sickness will not end in death. It is for the glory of God. This has happened to bring glory to the Son of God." Jesus loved Martha and her sister and Lazarus....

Jesus arrived in Bethany. There he learned that Lazarus had already been dead and in the tomb for four days....

Martha said to Jesus, "Lord, if you had been here, my brother would not have died. But I know that even now God will give you anything you ask."

Jesus said, "Your brother will rise and live again."…

Jesus felt very sad in his heart. He came to the tomb. The tomb was a cave with a large stone covering the entrance. Jesus said, "Move the stone away."…

So they moved the stone away from the entrance…. [Jesus] cried out in a loud voice, "Lazarus, come out!" The dead man came out. His hands and feet were wrapped with pieces of cloth, and he had a cloth around his face.

Jesus said to them, "Take the cloth off of him and let him go."

Sweet Dreams Devotion

This is a very unusual story. Jesus had just gotten the news that his friend Lazarus was very sick. Shouldn't he have hurried to Lazarus's house to heal him?

Everyone else thought so. But Jesus was not listening to what other people said he should do. He obeyed only his Father in heaven. So Jesus didn't go for three days, and his friend Lazarus died.

Mary and Martha were Lazarus's sisters, and they were very upset that Jesus didn't come in time to save their brother. In tears, they told Jesus that Lazarus was already buried in the cave. But Jesus told them to move the stone away from the tomb. In a loud voice, he called Lazarus to come out. Lazarus obeyed, even though he was still wearing the grave clothes wrapped around his body. Everyone understood that Jesus had power even over death. Then they gave praise to God!

Promise

God has given Jesus power over life and death, and one day everyone who trusts in him will live with him forever.

The Triumphant Entry

LUKE 19:28-37

After Jesus said this, he went on toward Jerusalem. Jesus came near Bethphage and Bethany, towns near the hill called the Mount of Olives. Then he sent out two of his followers. He said, "Go into the town you can see there. When you enter it, you will find a colt tied there. No one has ever ridden this colt. Untie it, and bring it here to me. If anyone asks you why you are taking it, say, 'The Master needs it.'"

The two followers went into town. They found the colt just as Jesus told them. The followers untied it, but the owners of the colt came out. They asked the followers, "Why are you untying our colt?"

The followers answered, "The Master needs it." So they brought it to Jesus. They threw their coats on the colt's back and put Jesus on it. As Jesus rode toward Jerusalem, the followers spread their coats on the road before him.

Jesus was coming close to Jerusalem. He was already near the bottom of the Mount of Olives. The whole crowd of followers was very happy. They began shouting praise to God for all the powerful works they had seen.

praise

Sweet Dreams Devotion

Let me ask you a question, Princess. If a king were to come into town, what do you think the parade would look like? Jesus, the King of kings, was getting ready to enter Jerusalem. But he wouldn't arrive in a beautiful chariot. He wouldn't even gallop in on horseback. No, Jesus planned to enter the city riding on a young donkey. He sent his apostles

Lord, I admit I like to get all of the **attention** sometimes. But you always thought of your Father and others. Help me to think more of you and **less** of myself.

Prayer

ahead to prepare the way. Jesus told them exactly where to find the colt and what to tell its owner. The apostles obeyed and found everything just as Jesus said.

So why choose a lowly donkey? Jesus was no ordinary king. Though he was God, he always humbled himself. He had come to earth to serve, and he never acted as if he was better than others. He has asked his people to serve him with the same obedient heart.

The Last Supper

MATTHEW 26:17-24

On the first day of the Feast of Unleavened Bread, the followers came to Jesus. They said, "We will prepare everything for you to eat the Passover Feast. Where do you want to have the feast?"

Jesus answered, "Go into the city to a certain man. Tell him that the Teacher says, 'The chosen time is near. I will have the Passover Feast with my followers at your house.'" The followers did what Jesus told them to do, and they prepared the Passover Feast.

In the evening Jesus was sitting at the table with his 12 followers. They were all eating. Then Jesus said, "I tell you the truth. One of you 12 will turn against me."

This made the followers very sad. Each one said to Jesus, "Surely, Lord, I am not the one who will turn against you. Am I?"

Jesus answered, "The man who has dipped his hand with me into the bowl is the one who will turn against me. The Son of Man will die. The Scriptures say this will happen. But how terrible it will be for the person who gives the Son of Man to be killed. It would be better for him if he had never been born."

feast

Sweet Dreams Devotion

The apostles couldn't believe it. Jesus said that one of them would hand him over to the men who wanted to kill him. Not only that, but Jesus said that all the apostles would run away and hide when he was taken. They all told Jesus that he must be wrong. They would never leave his side.

Who was wrong, the apostles or Jesus? You guessed it. Judas betrayed Jesus, just like Jesus said. Then the rest of the apostles got scared and left Jesus alone with his enemies. Even Peter told people in the crowd that he never knew Jesus.

Even though Jesus knew all his friends would make the wrong choice, he still loved them. God knows that we will sin too. But we don't have to be afraid of him. God still loves us. He just wants us to turn from doing the wrong thing so we can get back to being friends with God again.

PROMISE:

God promises to be faithful to us, even when we are not **FAITHFUL** to him.

Judas Betrays Jesus

MATTHEW 26:47-54

While Jesus was...speaking, Judas came up. Judas was 1 of the 12 followers. He had many people with him. They had been sent from the leading priests and the elders of the people. They carried swords and clubs. Judas had planned to give them a signal. He had said, "The man I kiss is Jesus. Arrest him." At once Judas went to Jesus and said, "Greetings, Teacher!" Then Judas kissed him.

Jesus answered, "Friend, do the thing you came to do."

Then the men came and grabbed Jesus and arrested him. When that happened, one of Jesus' followers reached for his sword and pulled it out. The follower struck the servant of the high priest with the sword and cut off his ear.

Jesus said to the man, "Put your sword back in its place. All who use swords will be killed with swords. Surely you know I could ask my Father, and he would give me more than 12 armies of angels. But this thing must happen this way so that it will be as the Scriptures say."

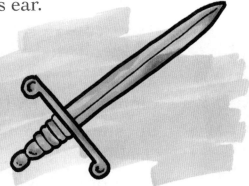

kiss

Sweet Dreams Devotion

Have you ever had a close friend suddenly do something very mean to you? It's hard, isn't it? You are not alone. Jesus had one of his own apostles turn against him. Judas decided to sell Jesus to his enemies for money. That had to have hurt a lot. Even though Judas decided to join the enemy team, Jesus did not change who he is.

The soldiers came after Jesus at night. At first, Jesus' apostles tried to fight back. Peter even cut off one of the men's ear. But Jesus immediately healed it. He told them that was not his way. He wanted to obey God the Father instead. He had come to earth to die for us, and he was determined to obey God all the way to the end.

Isn't Jesus the best friend we could ever have? Thank him right now for all that he has done for you.

prayer

Dear Father, please keep me from ever leaving Jesus' side. I want to stay close to him my whole life, no matter whether my friends turn against him or not.

Peter Denies Jesus

LUKE 22:54-62

They arrested Jesus and took him away. They brought him into the house of the high priest. Peter followed them, but he did not go near Jesus. The soldiers started a fire in the middle of the courtyard and sat together. Peter sat with them. A servant girl saw Peter sitting there near the light. She looked closely at Peter's face and said, "This man was also with him!"

But Peter said this was not true. He said, "Girl, I don't know him."

A short time later, another person saw Peter and said, "You are also one of them."

But Peter said, "Man,
I am not!"

About an hour
later, another
man insisted,
"It is true! This
man was with him.
He is from Galilee!"

But Peter said, "Man, I don't know
what you are talking about!"

Immediately, while Peter was still
speaking, a rooster crowed. Then the
Lord turned and looked straight at
Peter. And Peter remembered what the
Lord had said: "Before the rooster
crows tonight, you will say three times
that you don't know me." Then Peter
went outside and cried with much pain
in his heart.

Sweet Dreams Devotion

Peter was ashamed. He had wanted to be strong. He told Jesus that he would never leave his side. But when the guards came to take Jesus away, Peter grew scared. He followed Jesus from a distance, but he didn't want anyone to know.

Then several different people began to recognize Peter. First a servant girl asked him if he was one of Jesus' apostles. Two other men saw him and said he belonged with Jesus. Peter was too scared to tell the truth. He told all three people that he did not know Jesus at all! Then…the rooster crowed. Peter remembered that Jesus had told him he would deny him three times before morning came, before the rooster crowed. Peter was so upset!

Do you want to please Jesus all the time? Sometimes it's really hard to stand up for what we know to be true, isn't it? Ask Jesus now to help you stand strong for him, even when it isn't easy.

PRAYER:

Lord, my heart wants
to be strong and **TRUE**,
but sometimes the rest of me
doesn't seem to want to help.
Help me to always do what pleases **YOU**.

Jesus Is Crucified

P ilate's soldiers took Jesus into the governor's palace. All the soldiers gathered around Jesus. They took off his clothes and put a red robe on him. Then the soldiers used thorny branches to make a crown. They put this crown of thorns on Jesus' head. They put a stick in his right hand. Then the soldiers bowed before Jesus and made fun of him. They said, "Hail, King of the Jews!" They spit on Jesus. Then they took his stick and hit him on the head many times. After they finished making fun of Jesus, the soldiers took off the robe and put his own clothes on him again. Then they led Jesus away to be killed on a cross....

They all came to the place called Golgotha.... At Golgotha, the soldiers gave Jesus wine to drink. This wine was mixed with gall. He tasted the wine but refused to drink it. The soldiers nailed Jesus to a cross. They threw lots to decide who would get his clothes. The soldiers sat there and continued watching him. They put a sign above Jesus' head with the charge against him written on it. The sign read: "THIS IS JESUS THE KING OF THE JEWS."

Sweet Dreams Devotion

The story of Jesus' crucifixion is horrible and sad. How could people kill the man who spent his life healing them? Why did they hit him and spit on him and call him names? He was hit with a whip. His hands and feet were nailed to a cross. Everyone stared as Jesus died.

Why did God allow the people to be so cruel to his own Son? God the Father and Jesus his Son had agreed from the very beginning. Jesus was willing to pay the price for our sin. We deserve every bad thing that happened to Jesus. But Jesus took our punishment on himself instead. He then covers us with his perfect record. When we trust Jesus, God now sees his perfect Son, not our sins. It was a very painful price to pay, but Jesus paid it because he loves all people. God treasures you as his Princess and paid the greatest price to set you free to love him. What a wonderful King!

Praise

Jesus, you alone are good enough to pay the price for our sins. Thank you for going through so much pain and shame so I could be a part of your family.

Jesus Rises from Death

MATTHEW 28:1-3, 5-10

The day after the Sabbath day was the first day of the week. At dawn on the first day, Mary Magdalene and another woman named Mary went to look at the tomb.

At that time there was a strong earthquake. An angel of the Lord came down from heaven. The angel went to the tomb and rolled the stone away from the entrance. Then he sat on the stone. He was shining as bright as lightning. His clothes were white as snow....

The angel said to the women, "Don't be afraid. I know that you are looking for

Jesus, the one who was killed on the cross. But he is not here. He has risen from death as he said he would. Come and see the place where his body was. And go quickly and tell his followers....

The women left the tomb quickly. They were afraid, but they were also very happy. They ran to tell Jesus' followers what had happened. Suddenly, Jesus met them and said, "Greetings." The women came up to Jesus, took hold of his feet, and worshiped him. Then Jesus said to them, "Don't be afraid. Go and tell my brothers to go on to Galilee. They will see me there."

empty

Sweet Dreams Devotion

What a wonderful day! It had started out so sad. Mary and Mary Magdalene were going to Jesus' tomb to rub special burial spices on his body. But when they reached the tomb, the giant stone covering the entrance had been rolled away! Angels appeared and the soldiers guarding the tomb were so scared, they became like frozen statues who couldn't move. The angels told the women that Jesus had

Not even death can defeat you,
Jesus. You are truly Lord over **all**!

Praise

risen from the dead. Jesus was planning to meet them in Galilee. The angel told the women to tell his apostles so they would all get to see Jesus again.

As they went to tell the news, Jesus met the women. They were so happy! They worshiped him and then ran even faster to tell everyone the good news.

Jesus Goes to Heaven

LUKE 24:36-39, 45-52

esus himself stood among those gathered. He said to them, "Peace be with you."

They were fearful and terrified. They thought they were seeing a ghost. But Jesus said, "Why are you troubled? Why do you doubt what you see? Look at my hands and my feet. It is I myself! Touch me. You can see that I have a living body; a ghost does not have a body like this."...

Then Jesus opened their minds so they could understand the Scriptures. He said to them, "It is written that the Christ would be killed and rise from death on the third day. You saw these things happen—you are witnesses. You must tell people to change their hearts and lives. If they do this, their sins will be forgiven. You must start at Jerusalem and preach these things in my name to all nations. Listen! My Father has promised you something; I will send it to you. But you must stay in Jerusalem until you have received that power from heaven."

Jesus led his followers out of Jerusalem almost to Bethany. He raised his hands and blessed them. While he was blessing them, he was separated from them and carried into heaven. They worshiped him and then went back to the city very happy.

Sweet Dreams Devotion

Strange things were happening. Everyone saw Jesus die, but now some women said he was alive! Could it be true?

Two followers of Jesus were walking down a road talking about how confused they were. Suddenly a third man joined them and began to explain God's plan. He opened the Bible and showed them how all of the words talked about Jesus. It was God's plan to send his Son to earth to die for their sins. The men invited the stranger to their house for dinner. When he prayed and broke the bread, the men's eyes were opened.

At last! They realized it was Jesus all along! That might seem a little hard to understand. But Jesus did not look the same as before. Later Jesus appeared to his apostles. He told them he would send the Holy Spirit to give them power to spread the good news to everyone on earth. Then he rose into heaven right before their eyes!

PROMISE:

Jesus Christ is risen from the grave! He lives in heaven by God's side, praying for us and preparing a **PLACE** for us to join him one day.

The Holy Spirit Comes

ACTS 2:1-6, 14, 16-18

When the day of Pentecost came, they were all together in one place. Suddenly a noise came from heaven. It sounded like a strong wind blowing. This noise filled the whole house where they were sitting. They saw something that looked like flames of fire. The flames were separated and stood over each person there. They were all filled with the Holy Spirit, and they began to speak different languages. The Holy Spirit was giving them the power to speak these languages.

There were some religious Jews staying in Jerusalem who were from every country in the world. When they heard this noise, a crowd came together. They were all surprised, because each one heard them speaking in his own language....

In a loud voice [Peter] spoke to the crowd: "My fellow Jews, and all of you who are in Jerusalem, listen to me. Pay attention to what I have to say.... Joel the prophet wrote about what is happening here today:

'God says: In the last days
  I will give my Spirit freely to all
    kinds of people.
Your sons and daughters will prophesy.
  Your old men will dream dreams.
  Your young men will see visions.
At that time I will give my Spirit
  even to my servants, both men
    and women.
  And they will prophesy.'"

Sweet Dreams Devotion

Jesus' followers waited patiently. Don't you think it's hard to wait when you are very excited about something that's going to happen? They knew Jesus would keep his promise. At nine o'clock in the morning it happened! God poured his Holy Spirit out on all the believers gathered there. It looked like flames of a candle burned above each head, and they all began to speak in different languages! People around them could hear what they were saying. Everyone was amazed! What wonderful stories of God they were telling!

God was preparing his people to share the good news with people all over the world. By the power of his Spirit, he would reach people who had never heard about Jesus.

God has given us his Spirit too, if we belong to him. Be bold like the early followers and spread the good news: We have forgiveness and life in Jesus!

prayer

Dear Holy Spirit, please give me the power to live a life that pleases God. Open my mouth and speak through me to people who need to hear about you.

293

A Temple Beggar Is Healed

ACTS 3:1-10

One day Peter and John went to the Temple. It was three o'clock in the afternoon. This was the time for the daily prayer service. There, at the Temple gate called Beautiful Gate, was a man who had been crippled all his life. Every day he was carried to this gate to beg. He would ask for money from the people going into the Temple. The man saw Peter and John going into the Temple and asked them for money. Peter and John looked straight at him and said, "Look at us!" The man looked at them; he thought they were going to give him some money. But Peter said,

"I don't have any silver or gold, but I do have something else I can give you: By the power of Jesus Christ from Nazareth—stand up and walk!" Then Peter took the man's right hand and lifted him up. Immediately the man's feet and ankles became strong. He jumped up, stood on his feet, and began to walk. He went into the Temple with them, walking and jumping, and praising God. All the people recognized him. They knew he was the crippled man who always sat by the Beautiful Gate begging for money. Now they saw this same man walking and praising God. The people were amazed. They could not understand how this could happen.

Sweet Dreams Devotion

Have you ever worn shoes or sandals that didn't fit very well? They can make your feet very sore and make it hard to walk. This poor man in the story had never been able to use his legs to walk. His friends would carry him to the Temple entrance every day. He sat there and begged for money so he could live.

One day Peter and John walked by him. As usual he asked for money, but Peter and John stopped. They told him to look at them. So he did. He hoped they would give him some money. But they didn't. Instead they told him to be healed in the name of Jesus! He stood up immediately and began jumping around and praising God. Then I'm sure he went to find some shoes! Everyone who saw him was amazed at the miracle.

Do you need help with anything? Don't just sit there. Turn your attention to God. He's looking at you! Ask him to meet your needs and he will.

PRAYER:

Lord, please forgive me
when I forget to ask you for **HELP**.
Help me to see my need
so I can **ASK** you for healing.

Philip and the Ethiopian

ACTS 8:26-31, 34-35

An angel of the Lord spoke to Philip. The angel said, "Get ready and go south. Go to the road that leads down to Gaza from Jerusalem—the desert road." So Philip got ready and went. On the road he saw a man from Ethiopia, a eunuch. He was an important officer in the service of Candace, the queen of the Ethiopians. He was responsible for taking care of all her money. He had gone to Jerusalem to worship, and now he was on his way home. He was sitting in his chariot and reading from the book of Isaiah, the prophet. The Spirit said to Philip, "Go to that chariot and stay near it."

So Philip ran toward the chariot. He heard the man reading from Isaiah, the prophet. Philip asked, "Do you understand what you are reading?"

He answered, "How can I understand? I need someone to explain it to me!" Then he invited Philip to climb in and sit with him....

The officer said to Philip, "Please tell me, who is the prophet talking about? Is he talking about himself or about someone else?" Philip began to speak. He started with this same Scripture and told the man the Good News about Jesus.

eager

Sweet Dreams Devotion

Do you ever find it hard to understand the Bible? I think most people would admit that it can be hard to understand sometimes.

Once an Ethiopian man was riding in his chariot. He was reading the Bible, but he didn't know what the words meant. So God's Spirit told Philip to catch up with the chariot. Philip called to the man and asked him if he needed help understanding the Bible. The Ethiopian was glad to have Philip help him learn about Jesus. He was so excited about the good news that he asked Philip to baptize him.

When they found some water, Philip baptized the Ethiopian. Then Philip disappeared! God moved him to another city where he could tell others about Jesus. The Ethiopian praised God for all of Philip's help.

Whenever you need help understanding the Bible, ask God for wisdom. Then ask your parents or your Sunday school teacher to help you understand. God will teach you his truth through the Bible and through other believers.

Prayer

Lord, please put people in my life who will help me know and understand you more. Teach me through your Word and through your people.

Saul Is Blinded

ACTS 9:1-9

In Jerusalem Saul was still trying to frighten the followers of the Lord by saying he would kill them. So he went to the high priest and asked him to write letters to the synagogues in the city of Damascus. Saul wanted the high priest to give him the authority to find people in Damascus who were followers of Christ's Way. If he found any there, men or women, he would arrest them and bring them back to Jerusalem.

So Saul went to Damascus. As he came near the city, a bright light from heaven suddenly flashed around him. Saul fell to the ground. He heard a voice saying to him, "Saul, Saul! Why are you doing things against me?"

Saul said, "Who are you, Lord?"

The voice answered, "I am Jesus. I am the One you are trying to hurt. Get up now and go into the city. Someone there will tell you what you must do."

The men traveling with Saul stood there, but they said nothing. They heard the voice, but they saw no one. Saul got up from the ground. He opened his eyes, but he could not see. So the men with Saul took his hand and led him into Damascus. For three days Saul could not see, and he did not eat or drink.

Sweet Dreams Devotion

Saul thought he was serving God. He believed the Christians were bad people, so he worked hard to punish them. He had no idea that he was the one who was wrong!

One day, Saul was traveling to put more Christians in prison. Suddenly, a bright light flashed around him. Jesus himself spoke to Saul. Jesus told him to stop punishing God's people. The light blinded Saul. So his friends led him to the city where God told another Christian to take care of him. Saul told God that he was very sorry for his sins, and he stopped hurting the Christians.

God, thank you so much that you use boys and girls and men and women to serve **you!** Just like Paul, I want to serve you with my whole **heart**.

God gave him back his sight. Then Saul began serving Jesus with his whole heart. God changed his name to Paul. Paul became one of God's strongest messengers of truth to the world.

Do you always think you are right? Remember to follow God's Word, no matter how much you want to think your way is better.

Peter Raises Tabitha

In the city of Joppa there was a follower named Tabitha. (Her Greek name, Dorcas, means "a deer.") She was always doing good and helping the poor. While Peter was in Lydda, Tabitha became sick and died. Her body was washed and put in a room upstairs. The followers in Joppa heard that Peter was in Lydda. (Lydda is near Joppa.) So they sent two men to Peter. They begged him, "Hurry, please come to us!" Peter got ready and went with them. When he arrived, they took him to the upstairs room. All the widows stood around Peter, crying.

They showed him the shirts and coats that Tabitha had made when she was still alive. Peter sent everyone out of the room. He kneeled and prayed. Then he turned to the body and said, "Tabitha, stand up!" She opened her eyes, and when she saw Peter, she sat up. He gave her his hand and helped her up. Then he called the saints and the widows into the room. He showed them Tabitha; she was alive! People everywhere in Joppa learned about this, and many believed in the Lord. Peter stayed in Joppa for many days with a man named Simon who was a leatherworker.

alive

Sweet Dreams Devotion

Tabitha was a hard worker. She loved the Lord very much and served him by helping the poor and needy. One day she got very sick and died. Everyone that she had helped cried. Some of the men went to Peter, Jesus' friend, and asked him to come right away.

But what could Peter do? She had already died! Peter remembered that the same God who raised Jesus was at work in him too. He went to Tabitha's house and got down on his knees and asked

God for a miracle. Then he turned to Tabitha and told her to get up. She opened her eyes and got up immediately! Can you imagine how surprised everyone must have been—including Tabitha! Many people became Christians because of what God had done through Peter.

PRAISE:

God, nothing is
    too difficult for you.
I praise you
    because you are the God
who performs **MIRACLES!**

Paul and Silas in Prison

ACTS 16:25-34

About midnight Paul and Silas were praying and singing songs to God. The other prisoners were listening to them. Suddenly, there was a big earthquake. It was so strong that it shook the foundation of the jail. Then all the doors of the jail broke open. All the prisoners were freed from their chains. The jailer woke up and saw that the jail doors were open. He thought that the prisoners had already escaped. So he got his sword and was about to kill himself. But Paul shouted, "Don't hurt yourself! We are all here!"

The jailer told someone to bring a light. Then he ran inside. Shaking with fear, he fell down before Paul and Silas. Then he brought them outside and said, "Men, what must I do to be saved?"

They said to him, "Believe in the Lord Jesus and you will be saved—you and all the people in your house." So Paul and Silas told the message of the Lord to the jailer and all the people in his house. At that hour of the night the jailer took Paul and Silas and washed their wounds. Then he and all his people were baptized immediately. After this the jailer took Paul and Silas home and gave them food. He and his family were very happy because they now believed in God.

freedom

Sweet Dreams Devotion

Paul and Silas were in prison because they had healed a woman in Jesus' name and Jesus set her free. The jailors put their feet and hands in stocks so they couldn't even move. But guess what. Paul and Silas could still move their mouths! So they sang hymns out loud to God while the jailor and other prisoners listened.

Suddenly, God sent a big earthquake. It jolted the doors open and the prisoners' stocks loose. Paul and Silas could have run for freedom, but they stayed. They wanted the jailor to know Jesus more than they wanted their freedom. The jailor couldn't believe how kind they were. He invited them into his home, bandaged their wounds, and fed them. Then he and his whole family became believers and were baptized.

prayer

Lord, I want to trust you like Paul and Silas did. Even in a very bad situation, they sang praises to you. Help me to always be ready to sing praises and share your good news with others.

Paul's Shipwreck

ACTS 27:14-15, 18-20,
39-41, 43-44

A very strong wind named the "Northeaster" came from the island. This wind took the ship and carried it away. The ship could not sail against it. So we stopped trying and let the wind blow us.... The next day the storm was blowing us so hard that the men threw out some of the cargo. A day later they threw out the ship's equipment. For many days we could not see the sun or the stars. The storm was very bad. We lost all hope of staying alive—we thought we would die....

When daylight came, the sailors saw land.... So they cut the ropes to the

anchors and left the anchors in the sea.
At the same time, they untied the ropes
that were holding the rudders. Then
they raised the front sail into the wind
and sailed toward the beach. But the
ship hit a sandbank. The front of the
ship stuck there and could not move.
Then the big waves began to break the
back of the ship to pieces....

Julius, the officer,...
ordered everyone who
could swim to
jump into the
water and swim
to land. The rest
used wooden boards or pieces of the
ship. And this is how all the people
made it safely to land.

Sweet Dreams Devotion

The local Roman rulers said Paul had to go to Rome to talk to Caesar. So they sent him by ship along with a captain and many other prisoners. Along the way, the weather changed. Paul warned them that they faced death if they did not stop. But no one listened to Paul. That was a very big mistake!

Then disaster struck! A terrible storm arose and lasted for weeks. They threw almost all their belongings overboard to keep the boat from sinking. They thought they were going to die. Paul said they still had hope. He told them an angel had visited him in the night. God was going to save everyone on board if they listened to Paul. This time all the men obeyed. The ship itself wrecked on the shore and was torn to pieces. But God kept his promise and all 276 men on board lived. God continued to work miracles through Paul on the island where they landed.

PROMISE:

God always does what he says he will do. He **KEEPS** his promises!

Love

1 CORINTHIANS 13:1-8

I may speak in different languages of men or even angels. But if I do not have love, then I am only a noisy bell or a ringing cymbal. I may have the gift of prophecy; I may understand all the secret things of God and all knowledge; and I may have faith so great that I can move mountains. But even with all these things, if I do not have love, then I am nothing. I may give everything I have to feed the poor. And I may even give my body as an offering to be burned. But I gain nothing by doing these things if I do not have love.

Love is patient and kind. Love is not jealous, it does not brag, and it is not proud. Love is not rude, is not selfish, and does not become angry easily. Love does not remember wrongs done against it. Love takes no pleasure in evil, but rejoices over the truth. Love patiently accepts all things. It always trusts, always hopes, and always continues strong.

Love never ends.

always

Sweet Dreams Devotion

First Corinthians 13 spells out love in simple words. The first part tells us just how important love is. We can be the most amazing people with all kinds of gifts and talents. But if we don't have love, it doesn't mean anything.

Then God shows us what love is and is not. Love is patient and kind. It is happy with the truth. It protects, trusts, hopes, and never gives up. What does love not do? Love doesn't envy or show off. It isn't prideful, rude, or self-seeking. It isn't easily angered, and doesn't keep track of what people have done wrong. And it doesn't like evil.

God says that love lasts forever. That's why we need to take every chance we have to speak and act in loving ways. God alone can change our hearts to make us love like he loves us.

Prayer

Dear Lord, thank you that you will teach me how to love you and others well. Give me a heart to love like you do.

The Fruit of the Spirit

GALATIANS 5:16-18, 22-26

Live by following the Spirit. Then you will not do what your sinful selves want. Our sinful selves want what is against the Spirit. The Spirit wants what is against our sinful selves. The two are against each other. So you must not do just what you please. But if you let the Spirit lead you, you are not under the law....

But the Spirit gives love, joy, peace, patience, kindness, goodness, faithfulness, gentleness, self-control. There is no law that says these things are wrong.

Those who belong to Christ Jesus have crucified their own sinful selves. They have given up their old selfish feelings and the evil things they wanted to do. We get our new life from the Spirit. So we should follow the Spirit. We must not be proud. We must not make trouble with each other. And we must not be jealous of each other.

Sweet Dreams Devotion

If you plant an apple seed, what kind of fruit will grow from that tree? Do you think it might be oranges? What about carrots? No, that's silly. Apples, of course!

So if God plants the Holy Spirit's seed in you when you become a Christian, what kind of fruit will grow in your life? The fruit of the Holy Spirit!

You can't eat the fruit of the Spirit, but you can live it out. God's fruit in our lives shows love, joy, peace, patience, kindness, goodness, gentleness, and self-control.

When you are letting God's Spirit rule in your heart, you will stop putting yourself first. You will begin to love others because God loves them, not because of what they can do for you. As you learn to love God's way, you will find the fruit of the Spirit showing up in the way you talk, act, and think. God changes us from the inside out!

Prayer

Dear Holy Spirit, please love others through me so everyone can see your fruit in my life.

Write down some of your favorite Bible stories or special thoughts you want to remember.